To the girls at 'Bursley'.

Hope you enjoy.

Mike

Saturday

A Story of Terminal Hope

by Michael Messinger

Saturday

A Story of Terminal Hope

Cover design by Jacob Kubon.

Published by

splatteredinkpress.com

ISBN 978-0-9848542-9-5

Dedication

This Book is dedicated to Buddy, Matt, Josh, and Todd.
You fought the good fight and were
an inspiration to many.

To Emily, Alex, and Christian: You are my joys.

To my wife Deanne: I could never thank you enough.
I will love you always.

And to God: Sometimes I don't know why,
but I know You do. That is all I need.

Table of Contents

Questions, Questions, Questions

I don't pretend to have all the answers. In fact, I confess to have few, but do I have questions. Questions like, why is the Duckbilled Platypus a bird and a mammal? Why is the word Phonics not spelled like it sounds? What is the purpose of a mosquito? Why haven't the Cubs won a World Series in over a century?

I also have more serious questions, like why in the most prosperous country on earth do people live on the streets? Why has AIDS racked the continent of Africa, leaving so many children either infected, orphaned, or both? Why do thousands of children die of hunger every day when there is more than enough food in this world to feed them? Why does ethnic cleansing take place, taking millions of lives simply for the reason that people are of a different race?

Why are people struck with terminal illness? Why was I struck with a terminal illness?

My list of questions is unending and the answers remain as elusive as ever.

Yet I know someone who has all the answers. He goes by many names: The One, The Creator, The Alpha & Omega, Yahweh, The One Who Is, Was and Shall Be.

He knows what is going on in the furthest galaxy and what we had for dinner last night. He knows the make-up of the tiniest piece of matter, to the largest star in the universe. He knows the baby born in Australia and the oldest man in Europe. He knows why we are joyful at a wedding, and experience so much sorrow at a funeral. He knows us in our lowest lows and our highest highs.

He knows the answers because He has lived this life. He took on human form, and joined us in our day-to-day lives. He joined us in our suffering, suffered with us and for us.

Many people say this gives them peace. For me, it gives me hope: Incredible hope.

My hope with this book is not to provide you with answers, although you may find some. My hope is not to give you comfort through your suffering, although you may experience it. My hope is not to make you think that everything will be fine, although everything will be perfect in the end.

My hope is to show that when you suffer, there is someone who suffers with you. When you accept that truth, you will feel the true Hope of this universe. You will feel the true Hope of this life.

You will feel the true Hope of God.

A Century of Hope

I am eight years old and as I enter this humongous, white building, I get very excited. The smells are awesome: hot dogs, peanuts, popcorn, pop, even the sweaty people. I love it.

I buy the program with my paper route money and look at the names on the roster. All these players I have only seen on television, but I will see them for real today. This place had seemed so far away, but now, I am here.

The coach of my little league team lines us up to buy hot dogs and pop. The dogs are cold and the pop is warm. Awesome!

I walk up the stairs to our seats and feel a nervous excitement. As we get higher up the stairs, we step into the sun-light. The grey floors and the concrete walls below turn into an explosion of color. The blue sky, the bright sun, and the green field are right before me. Never in all of my eight years have I had a moment like this.

I take it all in: the workers working on the infield; the giant green scoreboard high above everyone; the rooftops across the street; and the people without shirts making lots of noise in the bleachers.

The outfield wall is made of brick covered in ivy. This is the only stadium in the league where the padding on the outfield wall is a living plant. Sweet!

We take our seats and watch our team get clobbered by the other team. Yeah, they got beat, but I don't care. I have found a place, and a team I love.

During the fifth inning, I see an old man seating fans in some of the rows near the field. He looks like he is at least 100 years old and I bet he has seen it all.

The Lost Saturday

Those of us who have grown up in the Christian tradition know the story of the death and resurrection of Jesus Christ. The Four Gospels, Matthew, Mark, Luke and John, all explain the events and characters of this story in great detail, and they all are similar in stating their accounts of the central point of our faith.

We know the story of the Last Supper, of Jesus praying in Gethsemane, of Judas' betrayal of Christ, of Jesus before Pilate, and of Jesus before Herod. We know the story of Jesus before Pilate again, Pilate's sentence of crucifixion, of Jesus being beaten, and having a crown of thorns mockingly placed upon his head. We know the story of the crucifixion, of Christ promising paradise to a thief crucified next to Him, and of the temple cloth ripped in two. We know the story of His burial, and we know the story of His resurrection.

Yet, the Gospels leave an entire day out of the story. That day was Saturday.

Philip Yancey wrote about this in his book The Jesus I Never Knew.

> The other two days have earned names on the church calendar: Good Friday and Easter Sunday. Yet in a real sense, we live on Saturday, the day with no name. What the disciples experienced in small scale –

> three days, in grief over one man who had died on a cross – we now live through on cosmic scale. Human history grinds on, between the time of promise and fulfillment. Can we trust that God can make something holy, beautiful, and good out of a world that includes Bosnia and Rwanda, and inner-city ghettoes and jammed prisons in the richest nation on earth? It's Saturday on planet earth; will Sunday ever come?

We have Good Friday. We have Easter Sunday, but we live in 'the day with no name.'

The only Gospel that mentions anything about that Saturday is the Gospel of Matthew:

> The next day, that is, when Preparation Day was over, the chief priests and the Pharisees went in a body to Pilate and said to him, "Your Excellency, we recall that this impostor said, while he was still alive, 'After three days I shall rise again.' Therefore, give the order to have the sepulcher (tomb) kept secure until the third day, for fear his disciples steal him away and tell the people, 'He has risen from the dead.' This last piece of fraud would be worse than what went before." Pilate said to them, "You may have your guard; go and

> make all as secure as you know how." So they went and made the sepulcher (tomb) secure, putting seals on the stone and mounting a guard." Mathew 27: 62-66.

The verses above make no mention of where the disciples, or any of Jesus' followers, were. They make no mention of what they were doing, what they were saying, or what they were feeling. So why didn't any of them write anything down? Matthew and John were both Christ's disciples, each one of the twelve. Mark was also a follower of Christ. Certainly, they knew what was going on that day. Matthew did record the above verses in his Gospel, but why didn't he record anything else? Why didn't anyone record the events of the day after Christ's crucifixion?

Maybe it's because Jesus' followers were good Jews and they didn't work on the Sabbath. There may be some truth in this, but I don't think this was the primary reason. The Gospels tell stories of Jesus and his followers striking ire in the hearts of the ultra religious Pharisees for doing good deeds on the Sabbath. They did not observe the Sabbath in the way that the Pharisees saw fit. It wasn't consistent with their pattern of behavior, or with their Rabbi's view of the Sabbath. Jesus taught them that the rules, regulations and outward appearance didn't matter as much as what was in a person's heart. Doing good on the Sabbath was more important than doing nothing.

Another possible reason might be because the followers of Christ were hiding. That would be understandable. They did not want to be the next to carry a cross down a road, ridiculed by citizens before dying an excruciating criminal's death. They hid because people knew who they were, and would associate them with their rabbi. Like Peter, they did not want to be associated with the man who turned Jerusalem on its ear, and then was put to death.

Or, the followers were struck with pure confusion. This was not how it was supposed to end. Their dreams had been dashed. Their Messiah, savior of Israel, their friend, was executed like a common criminal, and executed without putting up a fight. It was as if He accepted His fate and gave up. He was the Son of God. He could have stopped it, but He didn't. After three years of walking with Him, seeing Him perform miracles, and hearing Him teach through His parables, they didn't understand. After hearing Him allude several times to His death and His resurrection, they still didn't understand. He was not there to save their people from the clutches of the Roman Empire. He was there to bring grace and forgiveness to the entire planet. He was there to show people how to live a better life. He was there to be the sacrifice for all mankind. He was more than just the savior of Israel. The disciples didn't understand any of that. Many of us think we would have gotten it, but would we? After all, hindsight is 20/20.

Biblical Scholars tell us the four gospels were written years, maybe decades, after Christ's death. So they

could have recorded what happened on that
without fear, but they didn't. Maybe nothing
orded about that day, even years after the ev -, be-
cause the writers wanted their readers to feel what they felt. Their dream was dead, along with their Jesus. Maybe they felt like Jesus quit. Maybe they felt betrayed.

I am not a Biblical Scholar, but I think the followers of Christ saw that Saturday as one of the darkest days in their lives. They had lost their dream, their Messiah, their hope.

Going through my journey with brain cancer, I have realized that our lives are like that Saturday. We are stuck somewhere between captivity and deliverance, dark and light, evil and good. Just like Christ's disciples, we struggle to find hope.

A co-worker of mine, a practicing Jew, and I were having a conversation about religion. He mentioned a sect of Judaism called the Messianic Jews. This sect believes that Jesus was the Messiah, and He will return to save His people, much like Christians do. However, my friend discounted that belief. He said it was impossible for him to believe that after 2000 years, a loving God could allow us to wait for His return while the world continued to be plagued by pain, disease, suffering and death.

My friend forgot that Christ left us with that specific purpose: to bring the good news to the rest of the world. He left that mission in our hands. He commanded us to help those who are in pain, or are suffering, or are sick.

He commanded us to show love and grace. He commanded us to be His church.

Yet some Christians have the same attitude as my friend. After all, it has been 2000 years! Even through all of our human advancements, pain, disease, suffering, and death still exist. Have you ever met a professing believer that has this attitude? Or a believer who questions why our world is so screwed up when we have a loving God who could take care of it with a snap of His finger?

Believers who think that way live closer to Good Friday. They exist sometime early Saturday morning. They are hung over from their hurt, pain and sorrow. Many of them are so focused on the troubles of this world that that is all they see. If all they see is their friend's cancer, starving children, inexplicable wars, people's greed and violent crimes, they are blind to the fact that Sunday is coming. If all they see is their Christ crucified, then they have no hope for hope. They are in the darkness, and can see no escape. At best, they see God as a distant being that takes a hands-off approach to our world.

On the other hand, some believers can only think about the Resurrection. They are grilling steaks on Saturday night. They walk through life as if there is no pain and suffering in this world. They don't understand why people complain about their circumstances. They don't focus too much on Good Friday because it is too depressing. They believe the tomb is empty, so everything is okay. Even though they might have a bad day at the office, life is still good. They're saved. They believe there is nothing else to worry about. They know Sunday is coming.

Rob Bell addressed this in his book Drops Like Stars. In discussing Jesus' parable of the Prodigal Son, Bell made a point that this story has an odd ending. The story doesn't end with the older brother reconciling his issues of injustice with his younger brother, who has returned after squandering his share of his father's inheritance on high living and prostitutes. The story just ends. Or as Bell says, "Some things never get resolved." Bell then goes on to say:

> And when we try to resolve things too quickly or pretend that everyone is there when they aren't or offer hollow, superficial explanations ... it's not honest and it's not right and it's not real. It's not how life is.

That is my issue. My resolutions tend to be anything but real. I want everything to be all right. I want everyone to be happy, regardless of whether that is real or not. I lean too much toward Resurrection Sunday.

The problem with living too close to the cross, or too close to the empty tomb, is that we are missing the rest of the day. Our perspective on life is either tied to the pain and sorrow of Good Friday, or to the bliss and elation of Resurrection Sunday. If we live close to Resurrection Sunday, we have to recognize there is still sorrow, hurt, pain and suffering in this world. The wars, crime, and disasters that we see on the news every day prove it. If we live close to Good Friday, we need to realize that in the midst of this world's brokenness, there is still goodness, faith and love. There are too many good, forgiving, generous people in this world for there not to be.

My wife and I are great examples of people living on opposite sides of Saturday. She is a proud, card carrying member of Club Good Friday, and I am a fan of Team Resurrection. Our differences often reveal themselves in discussions like this one (paraphrased, of course):

> "Mike, I don't understand any of this. Why do children have to get sick and die? Why would God allow that? Why is there so much suffering in the world?" she says with great confusion.
>
> "Well, I believe God uses our times of suffering to bring us closer to Him," I say with confidence.
>
> "That seems cruel. Does God make us suffer just so we can get closer to Him?" She asks, thinking I would struggle with the answer.
>
> "Well God didn't create suffering. We did. It's called the Great Fall." I say trying to sound theological.
>
> "Well, that seems stupid. Why didn't Eve just say no to the serpent? Why didn't Adam stop her?" She asks with an indignant tone in her voice.

"Because honey, God created us with something called free-will. Adam and Eve chose to eat the fruit." Once again, I attempt to sound like I know what I am talking about.

"Well, I thought God sees all and knows all?" she asks this, laying her trap.

"Well, duh! Of course He does. He is God after all," I answer as if everyone should know that.

"So if He is all knowing and all seeing, then why did He create us with freewill if He knew we would sin?" She says with a smile on her face.

"That's easy. He did that because He wants us to show Him that we love Him," I say, thinking I am fortunate to come up with that answer.

"Well, if He wants us to love Him, then why create Freewill? Why not make us love Him?" she asks, seeing the wheels had come off my argument.

"Because, that's not how love works. You have to choose to love somebody. If you don't, it's not love," I feel as if I am back in the game again.

"Okay, say someone works in pediatric oncology, sees innocent little children dying every day, and says that God cannot possibly be a loving God and let all this

> happen, and as a result, doesn't love God. Is that person going to hell?" she asks, knowing she has taken the discussion to a whole other level.
>
> At this point, I made an excuse of having an important meeting in the morning and need to get some sleep.

Even though my wife and I approach life from different perspectives, we both suffer from the same issue. We are not seeing the rest of the story. We are both living in Saturday, but she is struggling to get out of bed in the morning, while I am living it up at night.

Sometimes our conversations were much more serious when it came to the 'realities' of my disease. My wife has an understandable fear of my dying, and her being left alone with the bills, the house, and the kids. She has said many times, she can't do this without me. I did my best to soothe her fears, even suggesting prayer, but her fears didn't go away. Spouses of people with terminal diseases know these fears. They can manifest themselves in depression, sorrow, and anger. My wife and I had heard stories of people who left their terminally ill spouses because they couldn't take the stress that the disease brings.

That is why, regardless of where one is in this day, living in Saturday requires one thing. Hope.

There was a cover of a local business newspaper that said '2009 Crystal Ball Edition' with a photograph of an old, covered bridge. At the end of the bridge, I could see the opening to the other side. That opening was filled with a bright, blinding light. It was so bright, I could not see through it. I had no idea what lay beyond. Superimposed on the left side of the photo was a green sign, similar to those on highways. It read HOPE LIES AHEAD.

Our Saturdays may seem like that old rickety bridge. It keeps us out of the rain and we don't have to slosh through the rapids below. The bridge gives a sense of comfort, and because of that comfort, the bridge seems secure. Yet at the same time, the bridge is risky, unsafe, and scary. Sometimes it comes with a lot of splinters, cuts, and bruises. Like that bridge, our Saturdays provide us with comfort and security, but at the cost of those pains.

Yet even when we get to the other side of the bridge, we still don't know what lies in the light. We may look back at the bridge and think, *it wasn't that bad.* It kept us above the river and out of the rain so we weren't getting soaked. However, that blinding light is right in front of us and it is bright and warm. Now is our chance to step into it, but that won't be easy. It will be risky and will require us to leave behind the comfort and security the bridge provided. Yet we believe what's on the other side of the light is so much better than what was on the bridge.

We believe, but we do not know, and that's the problem.

Our Saturdays are filled with bumps, bruises, sorrows, pains and sadness, but there is also comfort and security. Are we so comfortable with our Saturday, that we are frightened to let go? What will happen if we grab on to hope? In order to do that, we have to trust that what's on the other side is better. We need to let that trust guide us.

In his book, The Return of the Prodigal Son, Henry Nouwen said it well:

> It is the place of light, the place of truth, the place of love. It is the place where I want to be, but fear being. It is the place where I will receive all I desire, all that I ever hoped for, all that I will ever need, but it is also the place where I have to let go of all I most want to hold on to. It is the place that confronts me with the fact that truly accepting love, forgiveness and healing is often much harder than giving it. It is the place beyond earning, deserving, and re-warding. It is the place of surrender and complete trust.

Saturday is where we are. When we are confronted with the pain Saturday deals us, hope can seem as far away as the east is from the west. Yet hope in God is right there in front of us. Just like that blinding light on the rickety, old bridge.

Finding hope in God requires surrender to His love, justice and grace. It requires complete trust in Him. Whether we are closer to Good Friday, or almost to

Resurrection Sunday, if we don't surrender to Him and trust in Him, hope will remain as elusive as ever. Hope is what is needed to get us through this Saturday we live in.

A Century of Hope

I can't believe they traded our shortstop for this guy. People say he's good, but I don't believe it. He is so young and inexperienced. There is no way he's going to help this team. This is frustrating.

I have waited five years for this team to win it all, and they haven't even come close. Every day I watch these guys, and every day they lose. That other team in town is at least competitive this year. Maybe I'll switch sides, but that wouldn't be right.

A couple of my buddies and I catch the train and ride into the city. We head up to the El platform and ride it to the park. The journey to the field is going to be more exciting than the game itself. We're not worried about getting tickets because no one wants to see these jokers.

At least walking out of the concourse and seeing that beautiful scene before my eyes is still a thrill.

As I take a bite of my cold hot dog and then a sip of my warm soda, I run into Mr. O'Brian. He is the man that seats people near the field and he still looks like he's 100 years old. He has become my friend over the past few years, and I tell him how upset I am.

"Mr. O'Brian, they got rid of our shortstop to get this guy."

"Be patient. Let's see what the new kid can do."

So I do. I sit and watch my team stink it up again through six innings. It is so bad, I don't even want to get up and sing the seventh inning stretch. In fact, nobody else seems to either, but we do.

The kid takes his spot in the on-deck circle, and I roll my eyes. "This is a strike-out waiting to happen."

At that moment, Mr. O'Brian comes up to me and says, "This one is out of the park son, this one is out of the park."

I watch as he sizes up the first pitch and takes it. He seems to do that a lot. On the next pitch, he hits a three-run jack out onto the street. Ten thousand people stand up and cheer. Who is this kid?

Cruising Toward Depression

Our 10-year wedding anniversary was coming up in August of 2002. To celebrate, my wife and I decided to go on a Caribbean Cruise with another couple. They had been on a cruise before, and assured us it was a lot of fun. I needed that assurance when I realized how much money it was going to cost. It was our first time cruising, and we weren't sure what to expect. An entire week on a boat with thousands of other people? It sounded claustrophobic to me. And the thought of being trapped inside a cabin while the ship was rocking had me seasick before we even set sail.

Our experience, however, was much different than our expectations. We were amazed. Cozumel, the Cayman Islands, and Ochos Rios were our ports of call, and experiencing the different cultures was worth the price of the trip. We climbed waterfalls, swam with stingrays, and even did a little dancing at a popular Mexican bar. We went to James Bond Beach in Jamaica where they filmed part of the movie Dr. No. Somewhere there's a picture of me in front of a cave doing my best 007 impersonation. My friend and I drank $1 Red Stripes while our wives shopped in the Straw Market and it was the best shopping trip I had ever been on. Our days at sea consisted of lying around the pool, taking walks around the deck, listening to great reggae music, and sampling some fine Caribbean adult beverages. Yet nothing compared to the food. I had never eaten so well (or so much) before the cruise, and I have never eaten so well (or so much) since. Courses and courses of the most fabulous cuisine awaited us every night. The desserts were to die for. I visited the gym a few times to try to burn off those extra calories, but it was an exercise (so to speak) conducted in vain.

My wife and I had the time of our lives. I'm not sure if the saying 'to fall in love all over again' is true, but we came close. Nothing could have ruined are new found affection for each other. If there were clouds available, we would have been floating on them. Of course, we had our own private cabin, and, well... you get the picture.

Our new love affair continued when we returned home. Even our friends and family became sick of our behavior. We were like teenagers. We were in love all over again and weren't afraid to show it. To top it all off, we found out Deanne was pregnant (you know, that private cabin). We were expecting our third child. I wanted to name him baby Cayman, but my wife wouldn't have it. Probably a good idea, so we settled on Christian. Our summer of happiness continued.

When I experience happiness, I feel like I am on top of the world. Have you ever felt like that? Maybe it was your wedding day, or witnessing the birth of your child. Maybe it was when you went on a first date, or when your favorite team won the championship. Maybe it's listening to a good song, seeing a great movie, or reading a page turning novel. Maybe it's as simple as witnessing a beautiful sunset. Whatever it is, we all have those times of happiness. For me, it was falling in love again with my wife, expecting our third child, and feeling like everything was right.

A fuzzy period of time passed after that summer. My wife went back to teach, and I continued working at my job. As for the details, I don't remember much. Autumn passed and the next thing I knew, it was Christmas.

People that know me know that I love everything about Christmas. I love going to the mall, wrapping presents, decorating, listening to Christmas music, eating all the great food, and I love Christmas morning. I love reading The Night Before Christmas to our kids on Christmas Eve, and then the story of the birth of Jesus Christ. I make sure my kids know that is the reason we celebrate Christmas.

This Christmas was different, though. I wasn't feeling right. It felt as if there was this dark cloud above my head. When I looked at things, they looked ugly. When I tasted things, they tasted foul. When I smelled things, they smelled putrid. I couldn't sleep at night. I woke in the mornings in a sweat with my head in my hands, not wanting to get out of bed.

A few days before that Christmas, I was in our basement wrapping presents, as I do every year. I was watching It's a Wonderful Life and eating Christmas cookies. I should have been happy, but I wasn't. I felt emotionally horrible for no particular reason. I felt like the world was falling apart all around me and I had no control. I was depressed.

The word depressed is used a lot and has become one of those words that has taken on all sorts of meanings:

> "My job is horrible, I'm so depressed."
> "Man, am I depressed. My girlfriend broke up with me."
> "I can't believe they're canceling *The X-Files*. That is so depressing!"

Or my personal favorite,

> "The Cub's blew it again. It can't get more depressing."

Words like angry, hurt, disappointed, or frustrated might be better choices in these situations, but because the word has become so generalized, people use it all the time.

For me, I wasn't angry, hurt, disappointed, or frustrated. I was suffering from depression. There seemed to be no reason. My marriage, kids, job, and family were fine. In fact, everything seemed fine. There was no specific thing that made me feel depressed, but I did, and I didn't know why.

I somehow made it through the next three months, but it was rough. My wife was due with our third child in March, and I didn't care. When Christian was born, I didn't feel the joy I felt at the births of my two other children. Now don't get me wrong, I love each of my children equally. I would give up my life for any of them, but at the time, I felt lost and cold. Even with all the guests we had, the delivery room seemed empty. I wasn't engaged and it felt as if I wasn't there.

After Christian was born, my wife suffered from a severe case of post-partum depression. Timing is everything, isn't it? We went to post-partum depression classes together to help her deal with her feelings. What nobody knew was that I was suffering from my own depression as well. That April, I was scheduled to go on a strategic planning trip for the company I worked for. Previously, I would have jumped at that opportunity. It was an honor to be chosen to go, but I was too depressed. About two weeks before we were scheduled to leave, I walked into my boss's office and told her I had to back out. I used the reasons that my wife had post-partum depression, we had a child less than a month old, and I couldn't leave her in that situation. My boss sat there surprised with her mouth wide open. I couldn't blame her. She was counting on me and I potentially put her in a bad situation.

I ended up going, and because of that black cloud of depression over my head, it was one of the hardest things I have ever done. Attempting to stay engaged with members of the Board of Directors, the CEO, and my boss was extremely difficult. When I returned, I took a Mental Health day from work. Over the next few weeks the depression became worse. I struggled getting out of bed, going to work, and coming home. The only time I could find peace was when I was sleeping, and even that was a struggle. It became so bad, I started telling myself it would be much better if I weren't here. I thought about buying a gun, leaving the car running in the garage with me in it, or jumping off a bridge. I decided that overdosing on pills might be the most painless way to find peace.

Here I was, a thirty-three year old man, married with three children, raised in a Christian family, considering suicide. That wasn't supposed to happen.

Around that time, I had a conversation with a fellow Christian about the Behavioral Health profession, and the subject of suicide came up. I had heard growing up, that if a person commits suicide, he would go straight to hell because he wouldn't have time to confess his sin of taking a human life. (Try telling that to someone who has lost a loved one to suicide.) I told this person that a person couldn't be in their right mind if they committed suicide. They wouldn't have control over their actions and God would forgive them. My friend agreed, but really I was just trying to convince myself that it was true.

My family takes an annual Memorial Day trip to a remote island in the Straits of Mackinaw every year. This trip is usually restful and peaceful, but not that year. I woke up early one morning, saw the beautiful sunrise, and felt like taking the rowboat into the middle of Lake Huron and jump in the water with the anchor tied to my feet.

My depression became so bad, people began to notice. I was taking more and more sick days. People at work were asking me if I was feeling all right. Friends were beginning to wonder why I wasn't coming around anymore. My wife, mother, and mother-in-law all thought I was having an affair.

I couldn't let this go on. Either I was going to do something drastic, or I needed to get help. I began seeing a counselor and obtained a prescription for an anti-depressant. The medication helped a little, mostly with sleep, but the counseling sessions were a real challenge. I went to those appointments thinking the counselor would be able to figure out what was wrong. But I learned that counseling sessions are a two-way street. We need to be able to communicate why we think we are feeling the way we are. I was feeling this way for no reason. I became so frustrated, I attended just three sessions.

While all this was happening with me, my wife was still struggling with her post-partum depression. It was so bad; she took a leave-of-absence from a good teaching job. As a result, we made the decision that we were done having children. Not because we didn't love them, but because it wasn't worth the pain she was going through. We decided to get it done the easy way and I was looking forward to the surgery. The idea of spending two to three days recovering in my basement on the couch, hiding from the world sounded wonderful to me.

The summer continued and soon autumn was upon us. My wife and I drove to Kalamazoo to see a Western

Michigan University football game with some friends. After the game, we went to get some pizza. When we were finished, we walked to our car and I told my wife "I don't feel right." She kept asking me what was wrong and I said, "I don't feel right." Something was happening and it was more than depression. It was a physical headache-type pain- a sharp, stabbing pain right behind the bridge of my nose. It was as if someone was taking two screwdrivers, jamming them through my nose and up into my brain. I couldn't talk, see or think. I was steps away from being disabled.

Since the location of the pain was indicative of a sinus infection, I had an x-ray done of my head to see if it was an infection or not. The results came back negative: no sinus infection.

A few weeks later, we met some friends from Chicago at a local restaurant for dinner. While I was driving there, I had one of those headaches again. This one was so painful I felt nauseous. I pulled into the parking lot, stepped out of my car, and threw up. This was no sinus infection or migraine. This was something else.

I continued on for a few more weeks and dealt with the headaches, depression and the feeling of hopelessness as best I could. One day I came home from work and told my wife I was going to bed because I didn't feel well.

"No. We're going to the Emergency Room," she said. "Get in the car." I was feeling so horrible, I didn't argue. At the hospital, the physician ordered a CAT scan and an MRI.

At 2:00 in the morning, October 31, 2003, I was diagnosed with a Stage Four, Glioblastoma Multiform Brain Tumor. The tumor was located in the left frontal lobe of my brain. It had grown so much and so fast that it was pressing on the front center of my brain, causing the headaches, the nausea, and the depression. All that time I thought I was suffering from clinical depression. I never realized it could have been something else.

The doctor told us this was the worst possible brain tumor one could get and I had six months to live. My wife was advised to begin taking pictures.

This diagnosis sent everyone into shock. My sister-in-law remembered it this way:

> I drove home from the hospital wondering if I was in the middle of a nightmare. It couldn't be true. I knew there must be some sort of mistake. Cancer doesn't happen to my family. It certainly doesn't happen with a stage 4 label to a man in his 30's with a wife and three children. Where was God in this? Where was His goodness? I felt no hope. The doctors had spelled it out pretty clearly. Mike was going to die, and there was nothing any of us could do about it.

When my co-workers found out, they began crying. One of my sisters flew in from Montana, another from Taiwan. Friends we had broken relationships with began showing up. My best friend from college, who is calm, cool, collected, and laid back, was so upset he had to ask a co-worker what to do. He flew all the way from Arizona to come see me. My parents and in-laws were freaking out. My wife was freaking out. Everyone was freaking out, except me.

A Century of Hope

I am feeling a little nervous. Can this be happening? My buddies and I can't even catch a train to get down here. We have to hitch a ride from my friend's dad.

It is so busy, we are lucky to find a parking spot on the street. The crowds are huge! I have been a fan for six years, and I have never seen anything like this. We've never had to wait in line to get into the park.

I have brushed up on my history of this team in the last year. They have not been to the post-season since World War II. They haven't won the championship since 1908. That was four years before the sinking of the Titanic, six years before the building of Wrigley Field, and nine years before the start of World War I. How many people have been born and died since then?

This city is excited. Everybody is talking about this team. I can't believe it and neither can anyone else, it seems. Everyone is coming in to the stadium with a look of disbelief on their faces.

I grab my program and scan the names on the roster: they are all there. It's their best line-up in years.

The kid has proven me wrong. Since I saw him in that game a year ago, he has become a great player.

He ties this game twice at the end with two homers, and they go on to win. I bet they will name this game after him.

As I am leaving the stadium, I run into Stanley. That's Mr. O'Brian's first name.

"Stanley, I can't believe it. This was the greatest game I have ever seen. That kid is going to take them all the way!"

"You know, I do remember when they went all the way. I was eight years old."

That means he is only eighty-four. Not as old as I had thought.

"Yet, I don't think this team will make it all the way," he says.

What? Why is he saying that? I leave the stadium confused by Stanley's statement.

I watch them clinch the division on TV in Pittsburgh. They have made it to the post season for the first time since 1945. My brother and I are jumping up and down in my living room as if we have witnessed the greatest sporting event of all time.

They blow out the Padres in the first game of the playoffs, and beat them handily in the second game.

Then I watch them lose the third, fourth, and fifth games in San Diego. The Bull lets the ball roll through his legs. One game was all they needed. One game.

My heart is broken. Stanley was right.

Finding Hope

The diagnosis of a stage 4, glioblastoma multiform brain tumor is horrible news. The chance of surviving five years is two percent. Yet it was the best news I could have received. What? The best news? Yes, the best news. I had felt like I wanted to take my own life for a whole year. Before this diagnosis, I didn't want to go on. Nobody could help me. I felt like a worthless friend, brother, son, father, and husband. I felt like a worthless human being. I felt hopeless.

My depression brought me to my lowest point. Now I knew why. Yes, I had cancer. I had a death sentence, but I knew that I wasn't going to feel depressed anymore. A few hours earlier, I had arrived at my darkest hour. Yet God was there at that moment. He came to me when I had no hope. He was there when I needed him most.

They sent me home later that day with medication to help reduce the swelling in my brain. I was scheduled for surgery the following Monday. That Saturday, we spent the whole day with relatives, friends, and loved ones. We all went to the mall, joked around in the women's intimate apparel section of a store, and played with fake breakfast foods like three-year-olds.

A friend of mine from college showed up when he heard the news. He and I had a falling out years before, and hadn't spoken since, but we made our amends and had a great time.

My wife had a friend show up that she used to teach with. They had a serious falling out a number of years earlier as well, but they too made their amends.

Here I was, with a malignant tumor in my brain that could kill me within six months, and God was using it for good. Broken relationships and friendships were mended and reconciled. Good relationships and friendships were strengthened. Family members were brought together. I always believed that God made good things out of difficult situations, but had never experienced it. Now I had.

My surgery was scheduled for 3:00 pm on Monday, but it didn't get started until 8:00. While I was waiting, I thought it ironic that my first surgery would be a big one: brain surgery. I considered asking the surgeon: "Does anyone ever say your job is easy? After all, it's not brain surgery. Oh, wait. Yes it is." I decided not to ask him since he was about to operate on my brain.

The surgery lasted for three hours, and the surgeon removed about ninety-five percent of the tumor. He said there was little bleeding and he had had only one surgery before like that. He told my dad that was a good sign.

After the surgery, I was lying in a hospital bed with tubes coming out of my forehead, a giant question mark scar on the side of my face, and a portion of my brain missing. Some argued that that was no different than before. Everybody is a comedian.

When I was still half out of it from the anesthesia, my wife came in to see me. When they prepped me for surgery, they put these stretchy bands around my legs to keep them from moving. I have a vague recollection of telling my wife I wasn't able to drive home until they took them off. Apparently that received a good laugh!

I also told my wife that God let me know everything was going to be all right. I wasn't sure how, but He did. She has never forgotten that I said that. Either have I.

What had started with a cruise ship in the port of Miami, turned into a different kind of journey. Red Stripes in Jamaica had turned into brain surgery. Snorkeling off the Cayman Islands had turned into radiation treatments. Shopping in Cozumel had turned into chemotherapy. The conception of our third child had turned into countless MRI's. My journey had turned 180 degrees in the opposite direction.

Yet I felt better because God was with me. When I hit my absolute lowest, God was there! When I was in the midst of the greatest depression of my life, God was there! When I felt like I couldn't take one more step, God was there!

Was God with my wife and I when we were cruising through the Caribbean, living life in the lap of luxury? Yes, He was, but we didn't need Him. Why would we? We were on a luxurious cruise ship. We were eating the best foods, drinking the best drinks, and were waited on hand and foot. We were enjoying untold beauty on a daily basis.

As Americans, we live in the most prosperous nation in history and most of us have few needs. We may be stricken with the Keeping up with the Jones' syndrome, but most of us don't worry about where our next meal is coming from, whether we will have a roof over our heads or clothes for our kids. As a result, our need for God seems minimal. We may believe in God, go to church and even pray, but our need for God still appears small.

It was like that for me until a seven-centimeter piece of malignant matter showed up in the middle of my brain. My safe, comfortable, independent world suddenly turned upside down, like a loop on a roller coaster ride. One minute I was cruising along the tracks, and the next, I was looking at the world from a different perspective. I had no control, yet I remembered that I knew someone who did, and I humbly went to Him. When I did, I knew He had always been there.

Even though I have found hope, this journey has never been straight, mapped out, or well-defined. It has hills and valleys, twists and turns and sometimes turns me upside down. It is a journey that affects everyone around me, especially my wife and children.

One of my first hopes after the surgery was that I would get to see my kids graduate. After a while, my hope turned into seeing my kids get married. After that, my hope turned into seeing my kids have their kids. Then my hope turned into my wife and me driving an RV around the country volunteering for the Red Cross and handing out Bibles during our retirement years.

I hoped I was going to be here for a long time, but based on the statistics of the disease, that didn't make sense. I was given six months to live. Yet how long I live is not up to the doctors or me. It is up to God. He is the one who decides if the hopes I have are going to come true.

I believe God can deliver on my hopes, but no matter what my hopes are, my perfect hope is in God.

A Century of Hope

The kid is still playing second, although he's not much of a kid anymore. He is still an incredible ball player, but now there is a new kid. This one is lanky, slow, and has bleach blonde hair. He looks like a surfer, and he has little power. So what position does he play? First base, of course!

At least we didn't have to trade for him. We brought him up through our farm system.

As I watch this kid, he grows on me. As long as we have a second baseman with some power, it's all right that this kid doesn't.

Defensively, he is excellent. Offensively, he is a doubles machine. I can tell this kid is a real ball player. He plays pranks in the locker room, he smokes cigarettes on the bench, and he is patient at the plate. He has become one of my favorite players.

I am attending a game toward the end of the season. Usually, my team is ten games back at this time of year, but this year they aren't. They are in first place. They look like a team headed for something special.

I am comfortable with the crowds now. Ever since that season five years ago, this stadium has sold out. I don't mind because the atmosphere is so incredible.

My friends take their seats, and I run into Stanley. He still looks like he is 100 years old.

"Stanley, what do you think about this new first baseman? I know he doesn't have power, but this guy can slap the ball all over the field."

"He is a good player. In fact, he is going to be a special player."

"Yeah, I can tell. I think he is going to take us all the way this year."

"You know what, that's not going to happen."

"Stanley, what is it with you? You said this last time!"

"I tend to know these things."

They do make the play-offs, but I watch my team go one and four against the Giants. However, my new favorite player hits .647 in the series. People say he's special. I say he's amazing.

Dangerous Territory

In the movie The Shawshank Redemption, Andy Dufresne (played by Tim Robbins) is falsely accused and convicted of murdering his wife and her lover. He is sentenced to two life sentences for each murder to be carried out at Shawshank Prison. Being the only 'true' innocent person in the joint, he serves his time with hope. Even in the darkest times, he holds on to that hope in his heart. His new friend, Ellis Boyd Redding, or Red, (played by Morgan Freeman) wants nothing to do with hope.

Andy, with the approval from the warden, writes two letters a day to the state in order to get appropriations to help build a new library. Six years later, the state grants his wish. They send him $200, along with boxes of books and records for him to start the new library. After rifling through a box of record albums, Andy picks out one with an Italian woman singing like an angel, and plays it on the warden's record player. He has not heard music like this in years. At that moment, he decides to play the music over the speaker for the entire prison to hear. The reaction from the prisoners is priceless. Every single thief, rapist, and murderer in the prison is staring, mouths wide open, at the loud speakers. Not one is moving. They are all entranced by the sound of the angelic voice.

That stunt costs Andy two weeks in the hole, which is a week longer than most receive. When he returns, he sits down with his friends with a smile on his face. One of his friends asks him how he could be smiling, and he says he had "Mr. Mozart to keep him company." His music was in his head. After that, he and Red have this conversation:

> "That's the beauty of music. They can't get that from you. Haven't you ever felt that way about music?" Andy asked.
>
> "Played a mean harmonica as a young man. Lost interest in it though. Didn't make much sense in here," Red said.
>
> "Here is where it makes the most sense. You need it so you don't forget."
>
> "Forget?"
>
> "Forget that there are places in the world that aren't made out of stone. That there's a... something inside that they can't get to, that they can't touch. It's yours."
>
> "What are you talking about?"
>
> "Hope."
>
> "Hope? Let me tell you something my friend. Hope is a dangerous thing. Hope can drive a man insane. It's got no use on the inside. You better get used to that idea."

Red had been in that prison, trapped inside those gray, stone walls for so long, he had given up the thought of ever seeing the outside. Some might call his emotion apathy. I call it hopelessness. 'It is better to have loved and lost than never to have loved at all,' is a well-known saying. What would happen if we replaced the word love with hope? 'It is better to have hoped and lost than never to have hoped at all.' Sometimes this life can seem like a prison, complete with stone walls, but after a while, we get used to it. We get so used to it, that we are scared to hope for anything different.

Red looked at having hope the same as having a pipe dream. He knew he would never leave that prison. Those stone walls provided him with a sense of security. He had his routine every day, and it never changed. He became so insulated from everything on the outside; he didn't want to risk the idea that he would ever leave. He believed that thoughts like that would only serve to drive him mad. Why get his hopes up for something he knew wouldn't come true?

In my journey with cancer, I have met some people with the same attitude as Red. These people have labeled themselves as terminal and have accepted their fate, instead of giving it to God. They do not want to get their hopes up, just to have them dashed. They want to protect themselves from being disappointed. Some might say I am foolish for my hope of traveling the country in an RV with my wife, volunteering for the Red Cross and handing out Bibles after I retire. They might say I have set my expectations too high in such a horrible circumstance. They might say if my hopes are not met, I will only feel more pain and sorrow. They might say if I accept the situation I am in and learn to live with it, I won't be disappointed. Yet if I don't grab onto hope, how can I say I believe in a God who freely provides it? I must hope. Yes, it is risky, but I would rather 'have hoped and lost than never to have hoped at all.'

When I was diagnosed, my family and friends listened to the doctor's words. The mood in the room was somber. In less than a minute, that doctor delivered a message that changed our lives. My CT scan revealed a mass, which triggered the order for an MRI. The MRI confirmed I had a stage four, Glioblastoma Multiforme brain tumor. We had no idea what Glioblastoma Multiforme meant, but we knew what a stage four brain tumor meant. With a straight face, she told us I had no more than six months to live. Her words fell cold on our ears. They had no compassion, no feelings, and no hope.

I understand doctors shouldn't create false hope in their patients, a hope they know isn't true. That would be irresponsible. Science directed my physician to tell me that I had a two percent chance to live five more years. Yet at the same time, for the patient and his family, a hopeful message is crucial. When we heard this news, the shock was unbelievable and we needed something to hold on to. We needed someone to assure us that everything was going to be okay. For the patients and families, responses like this make an already stressful situation worse. Sometimes the way doctors say their words can sound cold and uncaring, and that coldness can make patients and their families feel angry, sad, and confused. Those words can take away their hope.

Yet real hope doesn't come from human beings, even doctors. Real hope comes from God. Instead of placing my hope in the science of medicine, I needed to place my hope in God. I had become so used to placing my hope in the experts of the day; I didn't realize these imperfect creatures would always let me down. Yet God wouldn't. Even if I didn't know what his plan was for me, I had to trust Him. I had to find my hope in Him and Him alone, even if that seemed dangerous. If I was afraid to grasp onto God's hope, to hold it for myself, to use it to get through my battle with cancer, I would have nothing but the bumps, bruise, cuts and pains that this life offers.

In the movie Contact, Jodie Foster plays the role of Dr. Ellie Arroway, an agnostic scientist who has spent much of her career trying to prove the existence of extra-terrestrial life. A message that she receives from the vicinity of the star Vega, provides her with instructions to build a machine; a machine designed to hold a human being.

When the pod drops, Ellie travels through wormholes to the star Vega. In her mind, she lands on a beach that looks like a picture she drew of Pensacola, Florida when she was a young girl. There, she sees her father who had died years ago. Her scientific mind can't explain it, but she saw what shc saw.

When she returned, Dr. Arroway is asked to testify before congress about her experience:

"Dr. Arroway, you come to us with no evidence, no record, no artifacts, only a story that, to put it mildly, strains credibility. Over half a trillion dollars was spent, dozens of lives lost. Are you really going to sit there and tell us we should just take this all on faith?" a congressman asks.

"Is it possible it didn't happen? Yes. As a scientist, I must concede that. I must volunteer that." Ellie says.

"Wait a minute, let me get this straight. You admit that you have absolutely no physical evidence to back up your story?"

"Yes."

"You admit that you very well may have hallucinated this whole thing?"

"Yes."

"You admit that if you were in our position you would respond with exactly the same degree of incredulity and skepticism?"

"Yes."

"Then why don't you simply withdraw your testimony and concede that this journey to the center of the galaxy in fact never took place?"

"Because I can't. I had an experience. I can't prove it, I can't even explain it, but everything that I know as a human being, everything that I am tells me that it was

> real. I was given something wonderful. Something that changed me forever. A vision of the universe that tells us undeniably how tiny and insignificant and how rare and precious we all are. A vision that tells us that we belong to something that is greater than ourselves. That we are not... that none of us are alone. I wish I could share that. I wish that everyone, if even for one moment, could feel that awe and humility and hope. That continues to be my wish."

As a trained scientist, Ellie had lived her entire life using only empirical evidence to prove the existence of everything. She believed that science and math tied the universe together. Yet she experienced a situation that threatened her previous beliefs. Through an experience she could not explain, she was able to grasp onto something. Even though she was putting her reputation as a scientist in danger, she was able to grasp onto hope.

Even those of us stricken by terminal diseases can live our lives to the fullest, yet many of us give up hope. We are told to cash it in, wave the white towel, and surrender to our illness, and we can do that, but not if we have the hope that Jesus Christ provides.

The hope that Christ provides says that regardless of our situation, suffering and pain, we still have life. Our life is a gift from God. He has a purpose for us. To help fulfill that purpose, God gives us hope, and we need to grasp onto that hope. Even if that hope seems dangerous.

If we don't grasp it, life becomes ultra-safe, ultra-comfortable, and ultra-plain. If we don't take that risk of grasping onto God's hope, we will never live our life to the fullest.

A Century of Hope

I want so much to pass my love for this team on to my new daughter. She is four-months-old, so of course, I decide it is high time to take her to a game.

I am glad she is only four-months-old so she won't remember my team stinking it up again. Still, they draw 30,000 people into the stadium. That's the unique thing about this team. Regardless of how awful they are, their fans are truly 'die-hard'. They are also loud. My daughter is startled by the noise of the crowd so my wife and her friend decide to take my daughter back to their house. They live right around the corner. Lucky, lucky, lucky.

My friend and I stay at the game. My favorite player that I found eight years ago jacks a home run. He isn't supposed to do that, but of course, I am fine with it. I also notice this other guy. He hits a home run as well, and he hits it far. I mean far. This guy might end up being a special player as well.

Even though my team stinks this year, they do end up winning the game. As my friend and I leave the stadium, he heads to the bathroom and I run into Stanley.

"Wow Stanley. Did you see how far that new guy hit that homerun? He could end up being pretty good."

"Oh, yes. He is going to end up being very good. One of the best this team has ever seen."

I think to myself that this statement is a little bold. "Really? That good?"

"Yeah. That good, but don't get too caught up in his play. There are reasons he is going to be so good. Reasons you will not be happy about."

"Um, Ok?" Sometimes I don't understand what Stanley is talking about, but he has never been wrong before.

Dreamers

The musical group Rush has a song called The Pass and the lyrics point to suicide being a result of one not having a dream. I believe there is truth in this. If we are not able to look forward to something, or even the possibility of something, then what do we have? We have where we have been, and where we are now.

The ability to look forward to something is what keeps many of us moving. Dreams don't have to be about being a millionaire, traveling the world, curing a disease, or being famous. Dreams can be as simple as getting a bonus at work, grilling a steak on the barbecue or seeing an old friend we haven't talked to for years. Dreams could be looking forward to a family camping trip, witnessing the birth of a child, Christmas morning or a wedding. The point is, without dreams, we can become depressed, and that can lead to suicidal thoughts, and maybe suicide itself.

Dreams are important, but there is a big downside to dreams. They are temporary.

When we achieve them, they last for a short while and then are over. December 25th always turns into December 26th. The steak gets cold and chewy after about ten minutes. The weekend wedding turns into Monday morning. That old friend eventually has to go home.

Dreams are temporary because they are our own. We create them. As mortal beings, by definition, we cannot create anything eternal. We do not have that ability. Don't get me wrong, we have the ability to create. The Creator after all, created us. There are too many paintings, poems, companies, ministries, sculptures, books, movies, plays, inventions, songs, and ideas to deny we have that ability, but we only have that ability because the Creator Himself gave it to us. As His creation, He designed us to create. Yet because of the fall, because of our sinful nature, because of our freewill, our creations are only temporary.

A television program on the History Channel depicted what the world would be like if the human race disappeared. I found this program interesting, but also sad. In one particular episode, the Statue of Liberty was shown buried in the mud of New York Harbor. It had become so decrepit and weak over the years that it broke apart and fell into the water below. All that was visible was her arm, the torch and her crown. A twinge of sadness struck me as I looked at that site. A great symbol of our freedom and liberty as Americans was deteriorating at the bottom of the sea. Why? Because it was temporary. It was a beautiful creation, but humans dreamed it and created it. That helped me understand why dreams are good to have, but never last.

As Christians, however, there is a much more dangerous side to having our own dreams than just being temporary. They might not fit into God's plan for us.

Some might say that is impossible. God gives us our dreams in order for us to pursue them, and help Him with His purpose. After all, God is God. His will be done.

The Bible, however, tells us something different.

> For we are God's workmanship, created in Christ Jesus to do good works, which God has prepared in advance for us to do. Ephesians 2:10

I never dreamt I would be diagnosed with cancer. My little dream had no room for a situation like that. It didn't fit. Yet it fit into God's plan. God had other ideas for me.

Even if my dream includes me doing work for God's kingdom, it's still my dream. I might spend my Saturdays at the soup kitchen helping feed the homeless because I believe that's what God wants me to do. It would be easy to believe that is what God wants me to do. After all, He commands us to take care of the widows, the orphans, and the oppressed. I might start a huge ministry that serves thousands of people and introduces them to the love and grace of Christ Jesus. After all, He commands us to spread the good news. I might write a book on my relationship with God so people can read it and live a more spiritual life. After all, He commands us to share the truth.

If my dream is to work for the Kingdom of God, how can my dream be wrong? Because it is my dream. Maybe God wants me to do something different. Instead of feeding the homeless, maybe He wants me to help a relative struggling with an eating disorder. Instead of starting a ministry, maybe He wants me to minister to my neighbor. Instead of writing a book, maybe He wants me to talk to an atheist friend.

He gives us that choice. Along with the creativity that the Creator gives us, He also gives us freewill. With that gift, we have the choice to allow God into our dreams, or not. We have the choice to allow God to show us his plan for us, or not.

Even if we believe what we are doing is helping to advance the Kingdom of God, it might not be what God wants us to do.

After creating Veggietales, selling millions of videos, creating an actual theatrical movie, and impacting the lives of children all over the world, Phil Vischer's dream began to crumble. His company, Big Idea, went bankrupt, and he was forced to auction everything he had created to the highest bidder.

In his book, Me, Myself, and Bob, Phil made a statement at the end of his ordeal about losing Big Idea:

> God could have spared me from the pain of Big Idea's collapse. He could have spared me from the consequences of my own mistakes and missteps. But He didn't. And it *wasn't* about 'God and Big Idea.' It was about 'God and Phil.' My ambition, my dreams, my misplaced sense of identity and value were dragged kicking and

> screaming up onto the altar. And now they were dead. Ripped apart like dragon skin.

Phil's dreams were dashed, but his hope wasn't. God was showing Phil what His plans for Phil were. Not Phil's.

This is a difficult concept for many Christians to accept. Why, if we were working for the Kingdom, would God take our work away from us and move us down a different path? Maybe, because in the middle of all of our work for the Kingdom, we forget that our relationship with God should be first and foremost.

Christian author, John Eldredge wrote about this in Walking with God:

> And so God must, from time to time, and sometimes very insistently, disrupt our lives *so that* we release our grasping of life here and now. Usually through pain. ... He thwarts us in our attempts to make life work so that our efforts fail, and we must face the fact that we don't really look to God for life.

God disrupted my life with a small, malignant tumor in my brain. It was painful as my efforts to achieve my dreams were thwarted. Yet, I realized they were just my dreams. They didn't fit God's plan, they fit my plan. Although I believed in God, my relationship with Him wasn't first and foremost. It was just there.

I realized through my circumstance, that God's plan for me was much different then I had imagined. Yet I trusted Him, because I knew He was God.

A Century of Hope

This year, my team is in the race. The last time my team had made it to the post season, I was nineteen. Now, I am twenty-eight, married, and the father of a beautiful little girl.

The player who hit the long homer last year is tearing it up. He is threatening to break the old single season home run record that has stood since 1961. And not just this player, but another player that plays for their archrivals. The fans can't get enough of this guy. He hits so many home runs; the team gives him a car.

The weird thing is that although my team is in the race, the fans seem much more interested in the home run record possibly being broken. This makes no sense to me. I don't even think the fans realize it has been ninety years since they won it all.

Because of some new league alignments, they win the wild card. It wasn't easy. They have to hold a play-in game at the stadium. Stressful, to say the least.

As a working man now, I am able to secure some tickets to this game. I go with a few buddies, and we grab our seats. We arrive early so I go get some souvenirs.

On the way back up to the concourse, I run into Stanley. He never seems to change.

"Stanley, have you ever seen anything like this? This guy can crush the ball."

"Quite frankly, it makes me upset."

"What do you mean? The record was bound to fall someday."

"Wait. You'll see."

Again, Stanley's statements confuse me more than help, but he has never been wrong before.

They do win the game. My favorite player catches the ball on his knees in foul territory, as if giving up a thank you prayer. It is an incredible finish to an incredible game.

I watch them on TV in the play-offs. Unfortunately, the boys from Dixie sweep them.

Whose Fault Is It?

A co-worker of mine experienced a deep tragedy in his family a few years ago. His son, who was weeks away from graduating high school, was killed in a car accident. I cannot imagine the loss he felt. Children are not supposed to die before their parents.

This co-worker is a believer and we talk to each other about our faith and the joys it brings to our lives. I count him as one of my confidants in the work place. He is someone I talk to when I have a bad day, or vice-versa.

At his son's funeral, when I made my way to him in front of the coffin, he grabbed me and wouldn't let go. He then looked me in the eye and said, "Mike, I am so angry right now. I am so angry with God."

"I would be to," I said.

Guess what? Lightning did not strike me, I was not infected with boils, and there were no locusts covering my house when I arrived home. Nothing negative happened because of my heretical remark.

In Shusaku Endo's book Silence, a priest named Rodriguez is asked to step on a fumie (a bronze image of Christ) to save the lives of others:

> 'It is only a formality. What do formalities matter?' The interpreter urges him on

> excitedly. 'Only go through with the exterior form of trampling.'
>
> The priest raises his foot. In it, he feels a dull, heavy pain. This is no mere formality. He will now trample on what he has considered the most beautiful thing in his life, on what he has believed most pure, on what is filled with the ideals and the dreams of man. How his foot aches! And the Christ in the bronze speaks to the priest: 'Trample! Trample! I more than anyone know of the pain in your foot. Trample! It was to be trampled on by men that I was born into this world. It was to share men's pain that I carried my cross.'
>
> The priest placed his foot on the *fumie*. Dawn broke. And far in the distance the cock crew.

Endo tells the story of a man full of guilt for having to step on this symbol of his Lord and Savior. Yet, because of his guilt and his belief that he would never desecrate his God, the One that he has 'believed most pure,' so many others have to die.

What if I were captured by some despicable people who told me they would kill other people unless I burned a cross, the symbol of my faith? These despicable people might tell me it is only a symbolic gesture, and "it is only a formality" and "It doesn't mean anything." I would be forced into a situation where I had the power of life in my hands. If I did not burn the cross, people would die. If I did burn the cross, people would live.

What a heart wrenching, gut wrenching situation. If I refused, I would have to live with the guilt of innocent people dying because of my refusal. If I agreed, I would have to live with the guilt of symbolically betraying my savior

Some might say they would refuse to commit such an act because, if the other people died, they would go to Heaven. Yet, what if those people were right there, staring me in the face? What if some of those people were women or children? Could I refuse?

That's why this passage from Endo was so striking. God Himself was saying, "Trample! Trample!" He did not send His only Son to earth to die on the cross and suffer hell for us not to "Trample!" Why would He pay such a price if we were to refuse His grace, His forgiveness, and His love? He was saying that was why He sent His Son. He sent Him to suffer for us and to be "trampled on by men." Only the Perfect One was able pay that price for us.

Notice the last sentence in Endo's passage:

> And far in the distance the cock crew.

This was a direct reference to Peter's denial of Christ. Peter had dropped everything in his life to follow Jesus who was his teacher and his rabbi. He had walked with him for over three years. He witnessed miracles that no other human being could perform. He even confessed that Jesus was the Messiah.

Yet listen to this transaction between Christ and Peter:

> Then Jesus said to them, 'You will all fall away from me tonight, for the scripture says: *I shall strike the shepherd and the sheep of the flock will be scattered*, but after my resurrection, I shall go ahead of you to Galilee. At this, Peter said to him, 'Even if all fall away from you, I will never fall away.' Jesus answered him, 'in truth I tell you, this very night, before the cock crows, you will have disowned me three times.' Peter said to him, 'Even if I have to die with you, I will never disown you.' Matthew 26:31-35 NJB

A few short hours later, however, that is what Peter did:

> Meanwhile Peter was sitting outside in the courtyard, and a servant-girl came up to him saying, 'You, too, were with Jesus the Galilean.' But he denied it in front of them all. 'I do not know what you are talking about,' he said. When he went out to the

> gateway another servant-girl saw him and said to the people there, 'This man was with Jesus the Nazarene.' And again, with an oath, he denied it, 'I do not know the man.' A little later the bystanders came up and said to Peter, 'You are certainly one of them too! Why, your accent gives you away.' Then he started cursing and swearing, 'I do not know the man.' And at once the cock crowed, and Peter remembered what Jesus had said, 'Before the cock crows you will have disowned me three times.' And he went outside and wept bitterly. Matthew 26: 69-75 NJB

Exactly as Jesus said.

My friend who lost his son was angry with God. That doesn't mean he denied he knew Him. Anger is a necessary emotion in a relationship, just like trust and love. People who are in true relationships express anger toward each other. I have a relationship with my earthly father and if being angry with him is not allowed, we don't have a true relationship. I love my father, and because I am angry with him, it doesn't mean I don't love him, believe in him, or have faith in him. It doesn't mean that he has no faith in me, doesn't love me, or doesn't believe in me.

Those who have experienced terminal illnesses, or unexpected deaths of loved ones, or a divorce, may be angry with God, and that is okay. Why? When you were a child, did you ever get angry with your father? I know I did, but when I look back on that time, I realize my father knew what he was doing. If you have children have they ever been angry with you? I know mine have, but it doesn't mean I'm going to stop loving them. It doesn't mean I won't discipline them, but it doesn't mean I wouldn't give my life for them.

If my father was willing to do that for me, and I am willing to do that for my children, how much more will my heavenly father be willing to love me? How much more will my heavenly father want to let me know that He knows what He is doing?

Yet, what if I didn't believe? What if all I believed in were the things I could see, feel, taste or smell? What if I was an atheist?

One of my favorite bands is Rush. Their lyrics for the most part, were written by their drummer, Neil Peart, a self-described agnostic. All one has to do is listen to songs like Roll the Bones or Freewill, with lyrics speaking about how life is just a game of chance, or how he chooses his own will.

Neil suffered a personal tragedy when his daughter was killed in a car accident driving back to college. His wife, grief-stricken, died a year later. Neil dealt with this tragedy the only way he knew. He took a motorcycle ride.

In his book, Ghostrider, Neil described what it was like for a non-believer to deal with such tragedy:

> On the short paved stretch of road leading out of town, I remembered riding the other way the previous night, feeling proud and exhilarated. Now I was frightened, weak, and weepy, truly dispirited, and as the paving ended, I found myself swearing out loud at the road, the rain, my life, and whatever Power might be responsible for all my bad fortune.
>
> But lacking the solace of faith, I also lacked anyone to blame.

The ability to be angry with God is only available to those of us who believe in Him. We can be angry at Him for our pain and suffering. As a result, those of us who believe have a great advantage over those who don't.

I have been asked if I became angry with God because of my brain tumor. My answer was 'yes'. The pure unfairness of this disease was enough to get me angry. I would see what this disease was doing to my family and friends, and would say to God, "how could you?"

There was a specific time when my family went camping with some friends about one hour from our house. I was on a particular chemotherapy that made me sick as a dog. I was so sick; I couldn't get off my couch. All I could think about were my kids camping without me. I felt helpless. My friend had to set up our camper for me, and be a dad to my children because I couldn't leave the house. I hadn't cried much through my journey, but that day my tears flowed. I hated that I couldn't be there for my family and I resented the fact that God allowed me to be struck with this disease.

Some believers may be uneasy with the concept of being angry with God. They may ask, "What about Job? He was angry with God, and how did God respond?"

God responded like God. Omnipotent, Omnipresent and Sovereign. He responded to Job's anger as the Creator of all things and gave him a five-chapter lecture on what it was like to be God: A 'you have no idea' type of speech. Yet, after His speech, God did the following:

> After Job had prayed for his friends, the Lord made him prosperous again and gave him twice as much as he had before. Job 42:10 NIV

When Job had reached his lowest point, he vented his anger toward God. As a result, Job had to listen to why God was God, and why Job was not. After that little lesson, God blessed him.

Getting upset with God is okay, as long as we know that God is God, and we are not. He may choose to bless us, like Job, or not. Yet He is God, and because God is always good, He always gives us hope.

A Century of Hope

I rest my head against the railing and can't believe what my eyes just witnessed. Five outs. Five lousy outs. That guy across the field in the stands interfered, and it was all downhill from there. I would hate to be in his shoes right now. It wasn't his fault. Our shortstop botched the play right after that, a play that could have gotten us out of the inning. That didn't happen. We went on to lose the game.

It isn't fair.

"Alright, I have had enough of this. Let's go drown our sorrows across the street," one of my friends says.

They all stand up to leave, but I don't join them.

"I'm going to pass guys. I'm so upset. I don't think it would be a good idea."

"So what are you going to do?"

"Stay here and mourn...again."

As they leave, I lift my head and view the scene in front of me. The visitors have cleared the field, after their little celebration. I know my team has a shot at winning the next game, but I am not confident they can get it done. This is such a huge momentum shift.

I see Stanley picking up garbage in his section. I force myself to my feet and go see him.

"Stanley, this isn't fair. We only had five outs to go, and we would have been in the series." I stare out onto the field.

"You of all people should know that life's not fair. How many times have you witnessed failure here?"

"Too many, but don't you get frustrated? I mean, when they're bad, it's frustrating, but not like this. Stanley, five outs were all they needed!"

I think for sure Stanley would have aged more after this game, but I guess it's hard to tell when you already look like you're 100 years old.

"Son, this is a strange game. It never turns out like you expect. You know, life is like that as well."

"I know. I know."

I walk out of the stadium with a slight glimmer of hope in my heart that they can win the next game. I watch that game, and of course, they don't.

A Question of Fairness

There is a saying that life isn't fair. Sometimes it is said to children who are whining because they are not getting their way. Or maybe it is said to a co-worker passed up for a promotion. Maybe we say it to ourselves after we see our neighbor drive down the street in a brand new sports car.

When we look at the inequities in our world today, that saying has different meanings for different people. Only eight percent of the world's population owns a car. How many of us own at least two? A twelve-by-twelve foot shed is considered a large house in Guatemala. Yet for many, owning a three bedroom, one bath ranch with a two-stall garage, isn't near their perception of large.

That raises a great point. Our perspective on fairness is just that: our perspective.

I don't know how many times I heard the saying "it's not fair" after I was diagnosed with a stage four brain tumor. A hard working married believer with three children shouldn't be stricken with a disease like that. I had to admit, I felt like that as well sometimes. I took good care of myself, and for my efforts, I had this disease. I felt as though I had been cheated and stuck with a raw deal. There were people who smoked, drank, didn't exercise and ate high fat foods that were walking around healthy. In addition, my wife was dealt a devastating blow and couldn't figure out how to deal with my disease and handle life at the same time.

There were times I felt like my children were being cheated out of their childhood knowing what was hanging over our heads. My mother-in-law remembered this:

> Cal and I went to Bauerwood Elementary School on Halloween to take part in the festivities with Emily and Alex. I believe Mike and Deanne were still in the hospital.
>
> We walked with the children in their parade and afterward, I sat next to Alex at his party. At one point, he looked up at me; his little face smeared with the remnants of a chocolate cupcake and said, "Wherth my dad?"
>
> At that precise second, the reality came crashing down around me. As I looked at that innocent, little smudged face, I thought, "How in the world are we going to tell these children?"

I think a lot about how my children have handled this. Their lives are not like their friends. They don't know if my brain-tumor will come back or not. That possibility will always be hanging over their heads. That affected my perspective on fairness, but again, that was my perspective.

There was a neighborhood fifteen minutes away from our house. I didn't go through that neighborhood often, but when I did, it changed my perspective on my raw deal. The neighborhood was one of the poorest in our area filled with crime where gunshots are heard at night, and gangs owned the streets. All I had to do was look at the rundown homes, the rusty beat up cars, and the abject poverty to see that I still had it pretty good.

Yet if someone living in that neighborhood were to go to Burundi, his or her perspective on fairness might change as well.

If we don't take that fifteen-minute drive to see how unfair this world is, it's no wonder we use the saying that life isn't fair as much as we do. The unfairness of this world is too striking to ignore, especially when were all born the same way. We all spent months in the womb and then were sent into this world. However, we had no control over when or where we were born. Immediately after birth, the unfairness began. Born in the suburbs of Chicago was very different from being born in the hills of Kentucky. Living through The Great Depression was much different than living through the 1980's.

My wife and I looked at our friends who were living their lives like 'normal people' while we went through each day not knowing if this tumor would come back. I looked at people I worked with, who seemed to complain about issues so menial, while I was concerned about seeing those dreaded tentacles on my next MRI. Many times I screamed at God, "It's not fair!" Sometimes I even screamed at God, "You're not fair!"

These accusations of God's unfairness raise an interesting question. Do we want God to be fair?

Andy Stanley addressed this question in his book, How Good is Good Enough?

> Despite the fact that we are fickle in our demands for justice, we sure find it easy to demand fairness from God. But that's only because of our distorted application of fairness. The truth is if you were to sit down and evaluate your divine demands, I think you would conclude, as I have, that you don't really want God to be fair. A truly fair God would give you exactly what you deserve and nothing more...

As Christians, we know this fact, but see it in a different way. The payment for our sinful lives is death. Eternal death. That is exactly what we all deserve. The only reason we even have access to eternal life is through God's grace. Interesting word, grace. A definition of grace is undeserved mercy that God gave to us by sending his son to die on a cross to give us a way to be with him in heaven for eternity, and not receive exactly what we deserve.

Grace is a free gift. God's one and only son paid the price for us. We don't deserve it, but we accept that free gift.

Jesus even speaks of God's unfairness. In Matthew 20, Christ's parable of the workers in the vineyard explains just how unfair God can be:

> For the kingdom of heaven is like a land-owner who went out early in the morning to hire men to work in his vineyard. He agreed to pay them a denarius for the day and sent them into his vineyard. About the third hour, he went out and saw others standing in the marketplace doing nothing. He told them, "you also go and work in my vineyard, and I will pay you whatever is right." So they went. He went out again about the sixth hour and the ninth hour and did the same thing. About the eleventh hour he went out and found still others standing around. He asked them, "Why have you been standing here all day long doing nothing?" "Because no one has hired us," they answered. He said to them, "You also go and work in my vineyard." When evening came, the owner of the vineyard said to his foreman, "Call the workers and pay them their wages, beginning with the last ones hired and going on to the first."

In this parable, which men were treated unfairly? An argument could be made for all of them. The men hired in the first hour could cry unfair. They put in at least ten times more work than those hired in the last hour. Yet, the men hired in the last hour were treated unfairly as well. They were paid the exact same amount as the men hired at the beginning of the day, but for only doing a fraction of the work. They were treated 'unfairly.' They received more than what they deserved.

As Christians, people saved by the grace of Christ, we are like those men hired in the eleventh hour. We are treated unfairly, but in a different sense than what we expect 'unfair' to mean. We deserve eternal punishment, death, and life separate from God. Yet God doesn't want that to happen. In that sense, God is treating us unfairly. He is giving us what we don't deserve.

God gives us something that, as human beings, we could never give. God gives us unconditional love. It is love that is not earned and has no strings attached, at all.

Romans 8:38-39 says, in my opinion, one of the strongest and truest statements in the Bible:

> For I am convinced that neither death nor life, neither angels nor demons, neither the present nor the future, nor any powers, neither height nor depth, nor anything else in all creation, will be able to separate us from the love of God that is in Christ Jesus our Lord.

For as much as we complain about life being 'unfair,' we really don't want God to be fair with us. His gift of grace, paid through the suffering, the blood, and the death of His son Jesus Christ, is an unconditional free offering.

I feel as if I have been treated unfairly. A tiny piece of malignant matter in my brain changed my life forever. I look at friends and family who aren't experiencing what my family and I are experiencing, and I cry unfair! Yet, in the end, with utmost humility and the highest gratitude I can possibly give, I accept God's gift, because life isn't fair.

A Century of Hope

Okay, last year didn't end up well at all.

The thought of being only five outs away from the World Series still stings. They were so close you could taste it. The electricity in the stadium during that series rippled through the entire structure. It seemed so surreal, but at the same time, nothing seemed more real.

Last year's loss hurt. It hurt even more than the loss in 1984. That team was one game away. Last year's team was only five outs away. In the end, it didn't work out. Something else is at work, and I cannot figure out what it is.

For all the years I have been a fan, my team never seems to be able to get it done. There is always some sort of catastrophe or bad luck they experience. Its inexplicable circumstances that leads to their demise.

This year is going to be different.

Our new pitcher is said to be one of the best young players around. He is everything a pitcher should be: tall, young, and a good hard thrower. Along with the cast from last year (including a new first baseman who happened to be on the team that knocked us out of the play-offs), this year seems to be promising.

I attend a game early on in the season. For the first time in a long time, I go alone. I am attending a conference downtown and today is the third day of the conference, so I decide to play hooky. Typically, the last days of these conferences contain too much socializing and not enough information of substance.

Besides, this new pitcher is starting today. He has great stuff. His mechanics are flawless, his pitches move well, and he has great composure on the mound.

In the National League, pitchers have to bat and I prefer it that way. That's real baseball. That's when strategy plays a role in the game.

However, it also puts the pitcher at greater risk of being injured. Our guy, this phenomenon, is rounding first and heading for second. He collides with a player from the other team and injures himself.

As I leave the game, I see Stanley.

"Don't say a word. I should have seen this coming."

"Yep!"

Move Toward the Light

People say they have seen God. Depending on your own thoughts on the Christian faith, you may choose to believe them or not. There was a time in my life when I chose the latter. If I heard somebody say they had seen God, I thought them naïve, foolish, or a little crazy. All I had to do was remind myself of Moses when he descended from Mount Sinai with the second set of Ten Commandments:

> When Moses came down from Mount Sinai with the two tablets of the Testimony in his hands, he was not aware that his face was radiant because he had spoken with the Lord. When Aaron and all the Israelites saw Moses, his face was radiant, and they were afraid to come near him. Exodus 34: 29-30 NIV

Moses' face became radiant after God turned his back on him so he could not see His face. If He had faced him, Moses would have died.

So, for me, hearing people say they had 'seen God' seemed strange. According to the Book of Exodus, they should be dead. Yet that was the Old Testament. For the ancient Jews, God's holiness was something to be revered, awed, and feared. Pious Jews wouldn't even speak His name. Only a certain priest, once a year, was allowed to enter the innermost section of the Temple where the Jews believed God dwelled. Members of his priesthood would tie a rope to him before he entered so they would be able to drag the poor priest's body out in case he died. To them, God was Holy Other.

Jesus changed the way we see and worship God. Consider His statement to the Samaritan woman at the well.

> "Sir", the woman said, "I can see that you are a prophet. Our fathers worshiped on this mountain, but you Jews claim that the place where we must worship is in Jerusalem." Jesus declared, "Believe me, woman, a time is coming when you will worship the Father neither on this mountain nor in Jerusalem. You Samaritans worship what you do not know; we worship what we do know, for salvation is from the Jews. Yet a time is coming and has now come when the true worshipers will worship the Father in spirit and truth, for they are the kind of worshipers the Father seeks. God is spirit, and his worshipers must worship in spirit and truth." John 4: 19-24.

Since Jesus' time, seeing God has taken on new meaning. Especially in my own life.

A month or two after I was diagnosed, a hawk took up residence in a maple tree in our backyard. I would see him from time to time, flying in and out of that tree. Hawks are beautiful and graceful birds, but they are fierce. Their white undersides camouflage them against the sky and they have the ability to glide on wind currents without flapping a wing. They do this to be unseen to rodents living on the land below. Once their keen eyesight picks up the sight of a mouse or chipmunk, the hawk dives to the ground, snatches up the poor creature, and moves on to an afternoon snack. There is grace and wild strength in this fantastic creature.

At this time, my wife was getting signs from God. Streetlights would turn on or off as she drove under them. Beams of light shining on snow crystals would stream hundreds of yards in the air from lampposts below. She even dug up a coin with a Bible verse regarding hope on it in while doing yard work. Once a complete stranger in the store came up to her and said she felt she had to give her $100. My wife broke down in tears and told the woman my story. She looked at my wife, with a tear in her eye, and said she knew she needed to give her the money. Her child had died from a brain tumor years before. Those signs from God to my wife were wonderful, but I was feeling a little left out.

I was in the bathroom when I saw the hawk again. I yellcd to Deanne, "Honey, I think that hawk is my sign from God." As soon as I said that, I knew I sounded somewhat desperate. A few seconds later, however, that hawk flew down from the tree and toward the bathroom window. It came so close I swear he was staring me in the eye. At the last second, he soared above the bathroom window, and over the roof of the house. Since then, hawks showed up at times when I was feeling low, scared or down. One time Deanne and I were driving early in the morning right before the sun had risen. We were going to the airport for another stressful trip to the Brain Tumor Center at Duke University. There we would receive the results of my latest MRI. As we were driving on the highway, a hawk flew right across our car, silhouetted by the early dawn light. I swerved to avoid it. At the Detroit airport, when our plane was taxiing to the jet way, we saw a hawk on a patch of grass between the runways, seeming to stare at us as we moved by. On our way from the Raleigh/Durham airport to our hotel, another hawk flew in front of our rental car, as if to say 'welcome.' Coincidence? Maybe, but I didn't think so. To me, the hawk had become the symbol of God saying, "I'm here. Don't worry. Everything will be okay. Trust me. I will never leave you."

Sometimes God shows up in our lives when our situations present an impasse. Or, to say it another way, when we are stuck. This doesn't always have to do with catastrophic events. Sometimes they aren't life threatening, economically disastrous, or emotionally damaging. Sometimes they're much simpler. They might be an opportunity for God to remind us He is always there. Since my diagnosis, my wife and I committed to creating special memories for our family. With the ever-present threat this horrible disease could come back, we wanted to make sure we were spending every waking moment living life to the fullest. A big part of this commitment included our family vacations.

We had planned to visit Walt Disney World during Christmas break. The place where dreams come true was also the place where meals cost more than the clothes on my back. This was the place where everyone was in character, the home of the mouse. We had planned this vacation months in advance, and were looking forward to getting away. Our kids at the time ranged in ages from five to eleven years old, perfect ages for Disney. However, the trip was almost over before it began.

At the airport in Grand Rapids, our flight was delayed. We were supposed to catch a commuter from Grand Rapids to Chicago. However, the plane didn't show up until about two and a half hours after its scheduled departure. On the flight to Chicago, I kept looking at the time and the map of O'Hare Airport, trying to figure out the quickest way to get to our next gate. When we came off the jet-way and into the terminal, the five of us ran as fast as we could. I knew we wouldn't make it, but I figured that after having laid out a lot of money for this flight, and the fact that it wasn't our fault, they would make sure to get us on another flight to Orlando. Unfortunately, about fifty other travelers had the same idea. Our connecting flight to Orlando had left, and the line to the ticket counter was long. Still we had three kids so surely someone would take pity on us.

After all, we needed to see the mouse! Of course, everyone else felt the same way.

We learned there was another flight going to Orlando that evening, but it was the last one. I stood in line at the customer service counter to see if we could get on that flight. After waiting an hour, I was told I would have to go back to the gate and get on the stand-by list. So I went back to the counter at the gate, waited thirty minutes there, and had the gate agent put all five of our names on the standby list. When I left the counter, the agent said she would be surprised if we would be able to get on this flight, and that the next flight for Orlando didn't leave until tomorrow evening, and it was booked. I walked away from the counter with my head reeling. The reality of the situation was sinking in. We weren't going to see the mouse. I thought about our luggage. Who knew where that was? I looked for signs to the car rental companies. It was late, but I could make the drive back to Michigan in four hours. The worst part was that I didn't know what I was going to tell my kids.

I practiced what I would say in my head. *Sorry guys. I guess it wasn't meant to be, but don't worry, we'll drive back home tonight. Besides, it's not that big of a deal. It's only the place where dreams come true.*

I looked at my family sitting on the seats in O'Hare Airport, exhausted, but ready to go to Walt Disney World. I prayed that God would somehow give me wisdom to tell them the news. I swallowed hard and headed over to them. At that moment I heard over the intercom "Mr. Messinger, please report to the counter."

What? Really? Did they get us on the flight?

I walked up to the counter and the kind woman said, "We were able to get you on the flight. They're not together, but we were able to get three seats as close as possible to each other."

Three seats? I had said I needed five seats. I knew God had a sense of humor, but this wasn't funny anymore.

"Sorry, ma'am. Did you day three seats? That's not going to work. I have five people in my party."

"Ohhhhhhhhhh," she said. Her fingers began to furiously tap her keyboard.

Great. Here we go again. I was going to have to tell my kids the vacation they had been looking forward to for months, the vacation we had saved up for, the dream vacation, was cancelled. I turned from the counter and looked at them. At that point, out of the corner of my eye, I saw the kind woman look at my family, and back at me.

"Mr. Messinger, let me try one last thing." Her fingers continued tapping the keyboard, her eyes following the shifting words and images on her terminal screen. After a couple of minutes that seemed like years, she looked up at me. Her eyes met mine. No smile or reassuring grin. This was it. I knew it was over.

"I was able to get you five seats on the plane."

What? Five scats? Did you say five seats? On this plane bound for Orlando, Florida? The home of Walt Disney World? The home of the mouse? The place where dreams really do come true?

After regaining my composure, I said "Thank you." She smiled and watched me go over to my family.

While we were standing in line to board, I looked at our row numbers on our boarding passes. We had rows two, three, and five. I turned to my wife and nonchalantly said, "Looks like we are sitting up front."

In fact, we were sitting up front. In the very front! In a land that might possibly be a little more magical than Walt Disney World. First Class!!

The seats were wide and made of leather. Leg room was abundant. The area was spacious. I sat in row five, my boys were ahead of me in row two, and my wife and daughter were across the aisle in row three. My wife turned to me and gave me the 'No Way' look. I winked at her and smiled. The meals were fit for kings, and the beverages flowed like milk and honey. The flight attendant came by with hot towels. I said I would take one even though I had no idea what to do with it. At that moment I thanked God. This was His doing, but He wasn't done yet.

After the meal, I stared out the window at the most beautiful sunset I had ever seen. At 30,000 feet, the sunsets look rich, and the sky shows colors of orange, red and dark purple. As the sun was setting, I saw three bright stars, lined on top of each other. I thought of God the Father, God the Son, and God the Holy Ghost. I leaned back in my seat, smiled and felt content. When we were approaching the airport in Orlando, the plane made a right hand turn, displaying the lights of the city to the passengers in the plane. I could hear my youngest son up front yelling to his brother, "Look, look. Isn't that awesome? That is so sweet!"

I looked over the first class cabin at my two boys, my sweet daughter, and my beautiful wife. I was blessed. As I took in the whole scene, my son's words echoed in my head. "That is so sweet!"

Indeed it was.

A Century of Hope

Sometimes, being a fan of this team means having to watch a lot of bad baseball. Okay, maybe not sometimes, but a lot of times.

I am fortunate to score a couple of tickets to the last game of the season with a buddy of mine. The team has long been eliminated from any chance of making the playoffs. Still, the experience of going to the park is exciting. Besides, we already know that the current manager is going to be let go at the end of the game.

Even though our team is absolutely out of it, they still draw 30,000 people to the game. Some things never change.

The game itself, even though it means nothing in the grand scheme of things, is still exciting. The score goes back and forth, and our team wins. I am glad I saw the game.

To me, it reminded me of baseball's elemental parts. It made the game seem more pure. They hit the ball well, manufactured some runs, hit their cut-off men, and didn't commit any errors.

My buddy says he has to catch the El back home. After he leaves, I see Stanley emptying garbage into a trashcan.

"Good game today, huh? I actually enjoyed it."

"I'm very glad to hear that. It's good to see that you haven't forgotten what this game is all about."

"What do you mean?"

"Well, winning and losing is important, but how you play the game is important as well. Don't forget, this is our pastime. If you don't enjoy the game itself, the way it was meant to be played, it doesn't mean anything."

"Stanley, you never cease to amaze me."

"See you next year?"

"Not if I see you first."

Stanley laughs. I think this is the first time I ever heard him do that.

Outside the stadium, my buddy calls me on my cell.

"Did you hear? They just released the general Manager!"

The winds of change had arrived.

Blessed Are The ...

Matthew chapter 5 contains The Beatitudes, a sermon Jesus gave on a mountainside to his disciples and the crowds that followed him. Some Christians might interpret The Beatitudes this way:

> "God blesses those who go to Church every Sunday."
> "God blesses those who tithe 10% every week."
> "God blesses those who work hard every day."
> "God blesses those who are strong."
> "God blesses those who memorize Bible verses."
> "God blesses those who don't memorize Rock n' Roll verses."
> "God blesses those who judge sinners."
> "God blesses those who don't drink or do drugs."
> "God blesses those who help themselves."
> "God blesses those who lead absolutely dull and boring lives."

Have you ever belonged to a Christian church that focuses more on the above than on the actual Beatitudes? Have you ever belonged to a Christian community that monitors every move you make? Does that sound like many of the Christian communities in this country? It does to me. That's the kind of Christian community where I grew up.

When I was a junior in high school, my family attended a legalistic church. Not only was this church legalistic, but there were smatterings of racism present. I heard one of my Sunday school teachers make some racist comments about people they had 'served' on a recent trip to Chicago. This church's pastor was a man who would berate parents in front of the whole congregation for not keeping their kids quiet and in control. He would preach his love for Christ, and at the same time, keep his judgmental eye on you. He was the kind of pastor whom you felt you had to be perfect around.

My parents invited the pastor over for dinner and they were carrying on a boring conversation about something. They asked me to be there, and listen to what he said, so I agreed.

"Why do we always have to get dressed up for church?" I asked him during dinner.

"Well, when I go in front of my God, I want to look as good as I possibly can," he said. As a cocky sixteen-year-old, my silent response was *whatever.*

When I think about his answer, that pastor was acting as some people did in Jesus' time. He was acting like the religious elite of Jesus day, like the Pharisees. He felt he had to be perfect to please God. He did his best to look, act, and dress perfect. The Pharisees self-perceived perfection created a prideful, pious class of people who looked down on anyone who didn't act like them. This pastor acted the same way.

Later, that pastor had an affair with a woman in the choir and the church let him go. My family continued going to that church for a few more weeks, but after a while, we left. My dad told me he was disappointed in the way the church handled that situation because they never once prayed for that pastor. They swept the entire incident under the rug.

A few weeks after that, two men (perfectly dressed, of course) approached our house and asked why we weren't going to their church anymore (keeping an eye on us as always). When they arrived, I was the only one home. I told them it was the whole situation with the pastor. They smiled, acknowledged the situation, and insinuated that they took care of the problem. I said, "No, that's not it. The problem is that no one in your church offered to pray for the pastor or offer forgiveness." They turned and walked away.

The irony of this was that these 'Christian Leaders,' were acting the exact opposite way Christ acted.

Jesus wasn't a legalistic preacher going from town to town telling people how to act so they could get into heaven. He wasn't a smiling, cleanly dressed man, carrying a lamb surrounded by children with a halo over His head. When He walked, he didn't have angels singing glorious choruses announcing His presence.

Jesus was someone very different. He was a longhaired (we think), bearded (we think), radical (we know), revolutionary (we definitely know) man, and a brilliant one at that. And He had a radical, revolutionary and brilliant message for this world.

That message turned the world upside down. It was as counter-cultural in first century Palestine as it is today, and the Pharisees hated it.

The Sermon on the Mount is a wonderful example of that message. The blessed weren't the ultra religious who tried to be perfect. They weren't the ones who dressed well enough for everyone to notice. They weren't the people who judged others. They weren't the ones who prayed aloud for the whole world to hear.

No, the blessed were the poor, the ones who were in mourning and the ones who showed mercy. They thirsted for justice. They were the ones who turned the other cheek, forgave, and accepted forgiveness. The blessed were the sinners. Take this example from the Gospel of Luke:

> Soon Levi held a banquet in his home with Jesus as the guest of honor. Many of Levi's fellow tax collectors and other guests were there. But the Pharisees and their teachers of religious law complained bitterly to Jesus' disciples, 'Why do you eat and drink with such scum?'Jesus answered them, "Healthy people don't need a doctor – sick people do. I have come to call sinners to turn from their sins, not to spend my time with those who think they are already good enough.' Luke 5: 29-32.

The blessed were also the sick, cast out and considered 'untouchable' by the religious elite. They were the lepers, the blind, the crippled, and the palsied. Some were even demon-possessed.

I felt somewhat 'untouchable' when I was diagnosed. Within three days, peoples' expectations of me changed. After my surgery, I took a walk around the block with my wife and some friends. A surprised neighbor called asking if that was Mike walking around earlier. She couldn't believe it. Yet while people's expectations of me changed, Christ's didn't. I was still His child, still His kid, and He still had a purpose for me.

Imagine some of our pastors and preachers hearing Christ say, "Hey, if you already think you're good enough, then you don't need me, do you?"

So if the religious elite didn't need Jesus, who did? The thief on the cross, the woman caught in adultery, the Jewish tax collector taking more taxes than needed, the prostitute who anointed His feet, and the Samaritan woman (considered an enemy of Israel) who was living in sin. They were the ones who needed Him. His message was for them. They were the sinners, the sick, and the oppressed. Christ's message of grace was for them.

To recognize this, all we have to do is read the first beatitude.

I own a New Living Translation Bible. When I read this Bible in small groups or Bible studies, some people get weird looks on their faces and because it's such a different version they aren't able to follow along. They usually tell me to stop and let someone else read.

However, this translation provided some clarity for the first beatitude. In the New International Version, Matthew 5:3 reads, "Blessed are the poor in spirit." In my New Living Translation Bible, it reads, "God blesses those who realize their need for him."

When I read this beatitude, I see Christ telling me to give up trying to be perfect. No matter what I do, I can't do it by myself. I know I can't be perfect. I know that I am not perfect, and as long as I draw breath, I never will be. I understand that all of the self-reliance in the world and all of the good works I do will get me no closer to God than when I am living in my sinful ways.

The Apostle Paul realized his need for God. He wrote about this in his letter to the church in Rome:

> I know I am rotten through and through as far as my old sinful nature is concerned. No matter which way I turn, I can't make myself do right. I want to, but I can't. When I want to do good, I don't. And when I try not to do wrong, I do it anyway. But if I am doing what I don't want to do, I am not really the one doing it; the sin within me is doing it. It seems to be an unpleasant fact that when I want to do what is right, I inevitably do what is wrong. I love God's law with all my heart. But there is another law at work within me that is at war with my mind. This law wins the fight and makes me a slave to the sin that is

> still within me. Oh, what a miserable person I am! Who will free me from this life that is dominated by sin? Thank God! The answer is in Jesus Christ our Lord. So you see how it is: In my mind, I really want to obey God's law, but because of my sinful nature I am a slave to sin. Romans 7:18-25, NLT.

Christ's message applies to all of us, because we are all sinners. Because of sin and because we are fallen human beings, terminal diseases can strike us at any time. Yet Christ had mercy on those struck with illnesses: the man who was blind, the man with leprosy, the woman who was hemorrhaging, and a man who had a seven centimeter malignant tumor in his brain. Christ had so much compassion that He would stop all of the 'important' things He was doing to heal them.

Jesus preached the Beatitudes to provide us with hope. Christ's message of love, forgiveness and grace remind us that we do not have to be perfect.

Those of us with terminal illnesses know, maybe more than others, that we are not perfect. Perfect people do not need a physician. They do not need to be saved and do not need grace. Only those who are sick and only those who are sinners do. Whether our sickness is physical, or we suffer from the sickness of sin, Christ still loves us. He wants us to go to Him, and he wants to offer us His grace.

For as much as we spend on health care, Christ has the perfect medicine for us, and it is 100% free. All we need to do is accept it.

A Century of Hope

The winds of change have arrived. A new manager, a new general manager, and a team with a new attitude.

The new manager brings a successful career record with him, and he has this team already playing well. People are amazed at how quickly they have turned their performance around.

The race has been close all year, but our team is still able to pull away and secure the division championship. The excitement is back at the old ballpark.

My family and I attend a game after they clinch the division. I sit back and watch my young children absorb all that is good about the game. My boys are busy trying to keep up with the scoring in the scorebook. They turn to me to ask for help, and of course, I oblige.

My wife and daughter busy themselves with people watching: always an event at this ballpark.

The team is playing very well today. They win the game, but I am more impressed with how they win. No errors, good starting pitching, excellent situational hitting, and a great relief effort to close out the game. They look solid.

After the game, I tell my wife I want to introduce her and the kids to Stanley.

"Sure, but the kids are anxious to get souvenirs. We don't want to have to wait in line long," she said.

"O.K., but when you're done, meet me down in that section." I point toward the area where Stanley works.

I make my way down the stairs, and see Stanley sweeping up behind the second row on the third base side.

"What did you think of that one, Stanley? They won, but they played great fundamentally as well."

Without a lot of excitement, Stanley said, "Yes they did."

"You don't seem too excited?"

"Well, you and I have been through this before. I'm afraid this isn't the year."

"Yeah. I used to think you were nuts when you talked like that, but I have learned not to doubt you."

At that moment, my wife taps me on my shoulder and asks, "Where's your friend?"

I turn to introduce them, but Stanley is gone. He must have snuck away.

Is There Anybody Out There?

I have heard some Christians say they have audibly heard God's voice and I have no reason to doubt them, but for most of us, it doesn't seem to work that way. That can be frustrating. After all, what's wrong with wanting the Creator of the Heavens and the Earth, the Alpha and the Omega, the One who was, is, and is to be, the Eternal Being, to be at our every beck and call and respond to our every question and need? Why can't the sky open up with a host of angels singing God's praises, setting the stage for God to grant our wish of a certain baseball team to win the World Series? Why can't God provide a map to where we lost our car keys? I jest, a little. Yet it does get maddening when we pray for things, important things, and it seems that God is too far away to provide an answer. Or that He might be somewhere else. Or, even worse, it seems He doesn't care. If we don't 'hear' from Him, we might begin to lose faith. The faith that tells us that God cares. If that happens, we are in danger of losing hope.

Maybe we need to look at this in a different way. When we pray for something important and God doesn't answer our prayers the way we want, it may seem to us as if He doesn't care. Yet how could God not care? We are His creation. He cares for ants in the anthills, moles underground, kangaroos in Australia and rats in New York. If He cares for the sparrows that fly through the air, how much more does He care for us? He knows how many strands of hair are on our head. He knows us better than we know ourselves. He created the entire universe, and God loves His creation. He loves the galaxy, stars, solar system, Earth, countries, states, cities, towns, neighborhoods, homes, families and us. He cares for us so much that He was willing to send His Son to the cross and suffer the eternal punishment we deserved.

Why? Because He loves us. Pure and Simple. For no other reason. His love is beyond our understanding. His love has no strings attached. It is 100% unconditional and it is free.

So, if He loves us so much why is our world so screwed up? Because our world has fallen. We were the ones that fell, not God. If you ever wondered who really killed Jesus, look in the mirror. You did. I did. We all did. We are sinners, plain and simple. I don't think one can become a Christian if he doesn't believe that. After all, if one doesn't think they are a sinner, why would they need Christ? They would be perfect. They wouldn't need to be saved.

When someone attends an Alcoholics Anonymous meeting, they introduce themselves as an alcoholic: "Hi, my name is Fred, and I'm an alcoholic. My last drink was 4 years, 53 days and (looking at his watch), two hours and 13 minutes ago." It doesn't matter when Fred had his last drink. He is still an alcoholic.

Being a Christian is the same way. Because we are Christians, it doesn't mean we aren't going to sin any more. It means that God's Grace has "washed our sins as white as snow." It doesn't mean that Jesus has to keep dying on the cross either. If we keep asking God for forgiveness each time we sin, we are asking God to continue to have his Son crucified. Christ crucified once is all that is necessary.

So if God loves us, then why, sometimes, doesn't He answer our prayers the way we want? It seems that either God is not listening, is too far away, or doesn't care. Yet that's not it at all. God has His own time. He has a plan, a purpose for all His creation, and a timetable that fits that purpose. He has a purpose and a timetable for us as well because we fit into His plan. So when God chooses to answer our prayer is up to Him, not us. How God chooses to answer prayer is up to Him as well. Not us. When He chooses to answer, He may answer Yes, No, or Wait.

I believe I have survived this long in spite of my brain tumor because of the power of prayer. I have met complete strangers in restaurants who have said they are praying for me. I cannot deny the power of prayer. My life is proof of that power.

Yet there was a time when I struggled with this. I knew other believers who had this disease and died. They had people praying for them as well. I felt a certain sense of guilt. What made me so special? I was no better than they were. Why was I still here but they were gone? Because of my guilt, I stopped going to cancer support groups. I was concerned people would be upset I survived while their loved ones didn't. I assumed God's answers to prayer were more random than purposeful, and if that was the case, why even pray at all?

I learned there was a very complicated answer to this. Ready? Because Jesus told us to.

"Give us this day our daily bread" is how Christ taught His disciples to pray. He told them to pray for what they needed. Jesus himself put His own teaching on display in the Garden of Gethsemane:

> He went on a little farther and fell face down on the ground. He prayed that, if it were possible, the awful hour awaiting him might pass him by."Abba, Father," he said, "Everything is possible for you. Please take this cup of suffering away from me. Yet I want your will, not mine" Mark 14: 35-36.

Notice how Jesus acknowledged that nothing was impossible with God, and notice how He prayed directly for what His specific need was. Then notice how He said He wanted God's will, not His. He was saying that God could grant His request, but only if it fit into God's plan. He used the exact template He taught His disciples in The Lord's Prayer. This verse was enough for me to know there was nothing wrong with praying for the things I needed or wanted. It also told me that even if His answer is 'no,' that God's will was still going to be carried out. Because God was good, God was love, and

God loved all of us. The fact that God's will was going to be carried out was comforting.

In the movie Bruce Almighty, Bruce (played by Jim Carrey), got an opportunity to be God. Yet when he learned that because of freewill, he couldn't make his ex-girlfriend Grace love him, he gave up. After deciding not to be God anymore, Bruce knelt down in the middle of a highway. He told God that he was done and wanted His will to rule his life. He was then hit by a truck, died, and went to Heaven. He saw God (played by Morgan Freeman) and had this conversation:

> "Am I -?" Bruce asks.
>
> "You can't kneel down in the middle of a highway and live to talk about it, son," God says.
>
> "But why? Why now?"
>
> "Bruce, you have a divine spark. You have the gift for bringing joy and laughter to the world. I know. I created you."
>
> "Quit braggin."
>
> "See. That's – that's what I'm talking about. That's the spark."
>
> "What do you want me to do?" Bruce says, holding Rosary Beads in his hand.
>
> "I want you to pray son. Go ahead. Use them."
>
> "Um, Lord, feed the hungry. And bring peace to all of mankind. How's that?"

"Great. If you want to be Miss America. Now come on. What do you really care about?"

"Grace."

"Grace. You want her back?"

"No. I want her to be happy. No matter what that means. I want her to find someone...who will treat her...with all the love...she deserved from me. I want her to meet someone...who will see her always...as I do now...through your eyes."

"Now that's a prayer."

"Yeah?"

"Yeah. It's good."

"It's good."

"S'good!!" they say together.

"I'm gonna get right on it," God says.

God gave Bruce two painful pokes to the chest, and yelled 'clear' both times. Bruce came back to life with the paramedics shocking him with their paddles.

Many people have asked me how I got through this horrible predicament. Initial reactions from people who heard I was given only six months to live ranged from shock to disbelief to amazement. After hearing about the severity of this disease and its devastating prognosis, they couldn't understand how I was able to function at all. To me, the answer was simple. It was prayer. More than doctors, nutrition, exercise or anything else, people petitioning God for my healing was the reason I have survived. It is because of people boldly going before the throne of God that I have hope for a normal, long life. If I recognize that God is God, He has all authority in His hand, and He has told me that He wants me to ask Him for healing, then why not ask?

For some, however, the real question in all of this is not whether God answers prayer, or when He does, or how He does. Their question is "Is God there?"

I mentioned that one of my favorite movies is It's a Wonderful Life. Along with many people, I see this movie as a story of hope.

In the movie, George Bailey (played superbly by James Stewart) has hit the low-point of his life. He has always wanted to be an explorer and travel the world. Instead, he finds himself drunk at a bar with a warrant out for his arrest. He berated his family because his life had ended up opposite of what he had expected. The richest man in town told him he was worth more dead than alive, and George believed it.

At this point, George doesn't take another drink. He wants to find out if "God is there." So George began to pray:

> God, oh God. Dear Father in Heaven, I'm not a praying man, but if You're up there, and You can hear me, show me the way. I'm at the end of my rope, and I... Show me the way God.

Only when George felt like he had reached the end of his rope, did he go to God. He wanted to know if God was there.

It wasn't as if God wasn't with George all the years he was chasing his dreams. He was there, right beside him, but George didn't feel the need to acknowledge God. Maybe George saw God as some distant being in heaven. Maybe George saw God as a hands-off deity.

George had to make that decision to go to God. When he did, he realized he had lived his life exactly the way God wanted him to.

Some of us are a lot like George. Our dreams may have been dashed, our health may have been compromised, or we may have suffered immeasurable losses. When we reflect back and begin to understand who God is, we may realize that we lived our life the way God wanted us to.

Because, after all, His will is perfect. Since it is perfect, we don't need anything else but His will in our lives.

A Century of Hope

Unbelievable. Well, actually not.

I am getting used to this. My team wins the division, but is one game away from being swept in a five-game divisional series.

The way they played during the regular season hasn't show up in the play-offs. Of course, the team they are facing in the play-offs pretty much owned them during the regular season. I should have seen this coming.

What is most disappointing, however, was the way they played. It was difficult to watch. Yes, they lost, but the quality of baseball played was not played at a championship level. The game wasn't even played at a fundamentally sound level.

I attend the last home game of the series, and watch them get beat. They are on their way to the other team's stadium, and of course, I know that isn't good. I start thinking that I am wasting my time with this team. I know there will never be another team I could care about so much, but I am almost ready to throw in the towel.

My friends ask me to go out for dinner, but I decline. I have an early morning at work, and need to get home.

As I reach around to grab my jacket off the back of my chair, Stanley taps me on the shoulder.

"Hey Stanley. Don't worry; I'll get over this one."

"Good, because next season is going to be special. One of the best in history."

"More special than '84? More Special than '03?"

"Well, from a certain perspective."

"You mean the quality of baseball, right?" I chuckle.

"Uh, no. I mean the number of wins."

"Stanley, you are a hard guy to figure out."

"Not really."

"Well, hopefully I'll figure you out soon. It's been nearly thirty years."

"Don't worry. You won't have to wait much longer."

I think this is a strange thing for Stanley to say.

Now What?

We have been struck by tragedy: an illness, the death of a loved one, a divorce, or the loss of a job. Whatever has happened, our world has been turned upside down. Maybe we want to get our life back to the way it used to be. I don't think that is possible. When we experience a traumatic loss, the onset of an incurable disease, the loss of a job, or a divorce, our life will never be the same. Grieving within itself is such a difficult and long process, there is no chance it won't change our life.

My grandfather died when I was fourteen years old. When I was younger, he was my 'best buddy.' We played catch, fished together, went to baseball games, and to White Castle to get those tasty sliders.

When I was around ten or eleven years old, he began to develop Alzheimer's disease. Soon, he couldn't speak. He had trouble remembering what had happened in the last hour, but he could remember events vividly from forty years ago. He couldn't drive anymore and he started urinating in his pants. One time my Grandmother fell and broke her arm. She was writhing in pain and angry with him because he wasn't able to help her. My younger siblings and I were the only ones there, so I ran to the neighbor's house to get help. That incident scared me. Another time he started a coffee pot on fire in our kitchen, and walked away as if it wasn't happening. His condition broke my heart.

When I was a freshman in high school, my Grandfather had a heart attack. After they admitted him to the hospital, they discovered he had lung cancer (he smoked all his life), and it had spread to his bones. He had received his physical death-sentence.

When I learned of this, I wasn't sad, angry, or upset. I showed no emotions. This man, who was my best friend, was dying in a hospital 200 miles away from me, and I had no feelings about it.

When I think back on it, he had died well before his physical death in 1984. He didn't play catch or fish with me anymore and we hadn't gone to a baseball game in years. I had lost my best buddy long before he physically died. I had mourned his death due to his Alzheimer's disease for so long, I had nothing left.

We had planned to visit him. My mother told me he was incoherent, and would most likely pass soon. Due to the drugs he was on, he didn't greet anyone with a smile. He was there, but he wasn't. I was glad she told me this. It would make the visit much easier for me.

Yet when I visited him in the hospital for the first time, he smiled. The dreaded effects of his Alzheimer's disease momentarily left him. My Grandmother couldn't believe it. She said it was the first time he had smiled since he was admitted. If only for a moment, my 'buddy' was back.

Eventually, my grandfather did pass away and at the funeral I showed no emotions. It was only the second funeral I had ever attended, and the whole event was strange to me. Looking at his lifeless body in the casket gave me no comfort. That was not how I wanted to remember him. I wanted to remember him holding that prize catch we caught right out of the lake and his cheering at the ball games. I wanted to remember him playing catch with me and downing those 'sliders.' That's how I wanted to remember him. So when I was at the funeral, I didn't react. I just went through the motions.

When we were back at the house, with all the friends and family eating and talking (another strange custom in my opinion), I walked around observing. It was as if he didn't exist at all, and people were ready to move on. I walked in the kitchen and saw my mother getting food ready. I then remembered my grandfather smiling at me in the hospital and I started to cry. My mother asked if I was okay and I couldn't stop crying. I wasn't crying over my grandfather's physical death, I was crying because I realized my life would never be the same. I missed my buddy.

That's the way it is. Grieving doesn't happen only after someone's physical death. We grieve losses all the time.

I believe part of the grieving process is learning how to bring good out of our losses. For example, if you:

- Are a woman who has had an abortion, maybe God wants you to council young, pregnant women who are considering their options.

- Are a father who has lost a child too soon in life, maybe God wants you to be there for other fathers who are in the same situation.
- Have suffered from substance abuse, maybe God wants you to counsel those suffering from substance abuse as well.
- Are a husband who has gone through a terrible divorce, maybe God wants you to help other husbands who have gone through similar divorces.
- Are a person diagnosed with an incurable disease, maybe God wants you to be there for other people who have been diagnosed with an incurable disease.
- Are a spouse of someone with an incurable disease, maybe God wants you to help those other spouses in your situation.

Notice the 'maybe's' in the above statements. Although they all involve helping others, and seem like logical things to do, they might not fit into God's plan for us. In order to understand what God wants us to do with our situation, we have to wait on Him. We have to approach Him in prayer, and ask Him for His will in our life; ask Him what He wants us to do with our cancer; ask Him what He wants us to do with our divorce; and ask Him what He wants us to do with the loss of our child.

Then we need to be silent and listen. We can't hear Him if we are not listening. Sometimes, He may clearly direct us down a certain path, or He may put situations in our way.

An atheist friend of mine was in the hospital due to issues with his leg. I went there to visit him, not expecting anything out of the ordinary. After all, it was only a problem with his leg, nothing life threatening.

When I arrived, we engaged in small talk. I learned what was ailing him, and how he was feeling. To my surprise, he had been in the hospital for what I thought was a very long time for his specific issue.

He started telling me how discouraged he was he couldn't walk, couldn't leave the hospital. He said he was in a tremendous amount of pain. He asked how I did it. I wasn't sure what he was asking. He said my ability, with three little kids and a wife, to handle my brain tumor in such a positive way, had amazed him.

At that moment I realized God had put him in my path to answer that question. As an unbeliever, he needed to hear it, but I felt like Moses. What was I going to say? How was I going to tell him why I was so positive without sounding preachy? So I trusted God, and just opened my mouth.

"It's God." I said.

"Hmm. I can buy that," he said.

Two words. That's all it took. Two words. I left his hospital room with a smile on my face. God had used me to reach him. I didn't force my friend to listen to me. I didn't throw fire and brimstone at him. I just answered his question honestly.

Sometimes, God may give a clear picture of what He wants us to do right away. Or He may take His time.

For me, I believe He wanted me to write this book. However, there was a time when completing that task became a struggle. Worry and doubt filled my heart and mind. I almost gave up. I was beginning to have serious doubts if I could get it done, or if I did, would it be any good. I had never written a book before. I was questioning whether this was what God wanted me to do. My discouragement became so noticeable, my wife told me to take the dog and go for a walk in the woods.

So I took that walk. It was quiet and peaceful, and the scenery was beautiful. Other than my dog pulling on her leash, I had no distractions. I began talking to God. I asked Him if writing this book was what He wanted me to do. I let Him know I wasn't sure, but I told Him I would stop writing if it wasn't His will for me. I told Him I would let Him use me in the way He wanted to use me. Not the way I thought He wanted to use me. I told Him I was throwing everything at the foot of the cross, and letting Him deal with it. Then I asked Him for His direction.

I heard nothing.

I walked back to my car, and drove home disappointed, believing I had to scrap months of work on what I had thought was His plan for me.

I woke the next morning before work, and began reading my men's devotional Bible. This Bible provides a devotional reading every day of the week. It also gives suggested passages to read before you get into the devotional reading. I turned to one of the suggested passages. Next to it, on the opposite page, was a devotion with the title Saturday. I did a double take. Destroying any regard for devotional reading etiquette, I began reading a different day's devotion.

It spoke of Saturday as being the day in between Good Friday and Easter Sunday. It spoke of Saturday as being a day where "we now live on a cosmic scale..." It was taken from the book The Jesus I Never Knew by Philip Yancey.

When I began writing this book, I knew I wanted the title to be: Saturday – A Story of Terminal Hope. That morning, it seemed that God liked that title as well.

I looked up from my Bible. I didn't have a mirror, but I'm sure there was a look of amazement, awe, and confusion on my face. I knew then my discovery wasn't a coincidence.

I had taken the walk the day before and laid it all out before God. I had surrendered my will to Him, and asked for His direction. Then I was quiet. The silence at the time was excruciating, but that morning, I realized God works in His own time. He told me what He wanted me to do in His time, His way and His voice, not mine.

For you, God might make you wait more than one day. He might make you wait a week, a month, or years before you understand His purpose for you.

Jumping into something we think we need to do to advance God's kingdom is noble, but we are still following our will, not His. In order to know His will, we have to be quiet and listen, because if we aren't listening, we will not hear Him. If we are listening, He will let us know, in His time, not ours.

A Century of Hope

Next year is here (again). I remember the words Stanley said to me last season, "Don't worry. You won't have to wait much longer."

I thought about that statement so much during the off-season that I didn't even pay attention to any of the off-season transactions or hot-stove gossip.

"You won't have to wait much longer." What could that possibly mean?

Stanley was right about one thing. My team is tearing it up this year. It is turning out to be one of the best regular seasons they have had in recent memory. Even better than last year.

I bring my family to a game in the middle of the season. The city is going nuts again over this team and its success. I am fortunate enough to get decent seats for all five of us. Of course, I reserve them as close as possible to the section Stanley works in. I am determined to introduce my wife and children to him after my failure to do so last year, and ask him about that statement he made.

During the sixth inning, my family asks me to get ice cream for them.

"Ice-cream? This is a baseball game, not a carnival."

"Please?" they all ask in unison.

As I walk back to our seats from the concession stand, I run into Stanley. It strikes me strange that every time I see him no one else I know is around. Ever since that first game I attended some thirty years ago, none of my teammates, buddies, or family have been around when I run into him.

"Hi Stanley. Looks like you were right again. They are having one of the best seasons in a long time. How do you know these things?"

"Oh, you wouldn't believe me if I told you."

"Well, I've known you for about three decades now, and everything you've said about this team and its players has come true. Why wouldn't I believe you?"

"I don't think you are ready for me to tell you yet."

"Okay, that's the second strange thing you have said to me in two seasons. What's up, Stanley?"

Stanley gives me a deep look he has never given me before.

The One Conclusion

I grew up in a Christian home. We had issues like all families do, but the environment was still safe and loving. I was taught to believe in God, in Jesus, and to tell people about Him whenever I had the chance. And I will say I accomplished all of that except for telling people about Him. Either way, I did believe in God. However, some legalistic teaching I had to endure tainted my view of Christianity.

For one of my birthdays, my parents bought me a rock n' roll record. There were no lyrics on the record considered dirty or offensive. I brought the album to my Baptist Christian school to show my friends, and one of them said "Yuck!" He didn't even look at the band name, album cover, or lyrics. He just assumed that since it was a rock album, his response was right.

I attended that school from kindergarten through eighth grade, and it molded me. Even though I listened to rock music on the side, I still learned a lot about being polite, to speak only when spoken to, and to respect my elders. I memorized the books of the Bible (the names of the books, not every single word), sang Christian songs, and was able to site scripture verse by memory. It was all I knew. I knew if I obeyed what they taught me, I was on my way to heaven.

Since then, however, I realized I was not taught the full story of Jesus.

I was taught we were living in the last days. With dark and ominous voices, pastors would deliver sermons filled with fire and brimstone. Leaning over the podium they would preach the Book of Revelations by speaking of beasts with multiple heads, the anti-Christ, the number of the beast, the great tribulation, wars and earthquakes, and a giant lake of fire. Talk about giving a kid nightmares. This wasn't some fictional horror story. This was real. This was going to happen in our lifetime.

Those sermons were designed to put people into a state of fear and scare them toward Jesus. Those sermons never taught me what grace was. I was never taught the Book of Revelation was a spiritual revelation of Jesus Christ. I was taught that if I behaved and was good, everything would be all right. Jesus was returning soon, and if he caught me sinning, I was in trouble. I was never taught the Bible was a story of God's hope and His plan to redeem the world.

I was taught Jesus was physically crucified, died and then rose from the grave three days later. I never realized the significance of spiritual darkness that took place on Good Friday.

I knew Jesus was crucified with two criminals on both sides of Him. I never learned the Roman Empire crucified people on a regular basis.

I grew up with many judgmental people, but learned later that Christ commanded us not to judge others.

I learned not to associate with sinners, but later, realized everyone was in sin. The rash of television pastor scandals at the time proved it. Even those pastors with the dark, ominous voices were in sin. We all were in sin. So why was being good so important? Weren't the sinners the people drawn to Christ?

All of those teachings affected my view of Christianity. They began to create serious doubts. Some almost turned me away from my faith.

One of those doubts was that Christ's crucifixion didn't seem so unique anymore. If the Romans were crucifying thousands of people, why was His crucifixion so different? All it took was a change of church to get my answer.

After my wife and I were married, we began attending her family's Lutheran church. At the time, my spiritual report card had a giant red 'F' for everyone to see.

At first, I thought the rituals and the customs of this church were very strange. The robes the pastors wore struck me as odd. I thought all pastors wore suits and ties. I wasn't used to walking to the front of the church every Sunday to take communion, and was shocked that they served real wine and not grape juice. I had attended a Baptist church and remembered no baptisms, yet I saw babies baptized regularly at my wife's church. I wasn't used to saying the Lord's Prayer every week, remembering from my childhood only prayers hurling guilt trips at people to come up to the alter and confess their sins.

Yet, the hardest thing to get used to at this church was the Good Friday service. In my upbringing, Good Friday was skimmed over so we could get to Easter. I couldn't understand why so much focus was given to Christ's death and burial. After all, Easter was why we believed, wasn't it?

These Good Friday services were always very quiet, and as they went along, the lights would be dimmed in succession. The windows were covered with black drapes, giving the sanctuary a look and feel of total darkness. At the end of the service, one lone woman in the back of the church would sing Were You There. After her haunting version of the hymn concluded, the pastor conducting the service would slam shut the Bible so hard people in the congregation would jump. The slamming of the Bible was to signify the stone rolling over the tomb that closed the door on Christ's grave. When the service was over, no one spoke. We walked to our vehicles in silence and drove home. It was a solemn experience.

There was a particular Good Friday service that marked a turning point in my life. I now count it as a catalyst for my second conversion. The pastor conducting the service spoke of the crucifixion in terms I had never heard before. He stated that Christ's crucifixion was more than just a physical death. When He was crucified, Christ suffered hell.

When he said that, my initial reaction was shock. *Jesus suffered hell? That can't be. I know He died on the cross, but suffered hell? How? He was there on the cross the whole time!*

I recalled a fuzzy memory from my youth of Christ saying on the cross, "My God, my God, why have you forsaken me?" When I was younger, no real meaning was ever given to it. Yet as I processed that statement, I realized what I had been missing all along.

God had left Jesus. God had separated Himself from His one and only Son.

My visions of hell began to melt away. Stories of deep caverns with flowing lava, demons torturing the unfortunate, and people burning alive for eternity in a lake of fire began to flee my mind. Hell was not that at all.

Hell was being separated from God. On the cross, Jesus was separated from God.

In his book, Blue Like Jazz, Donald Miller described what he thought hell would be like:

> There was once a man named Don Astronaut. Don Astronaut lived on a space station out in space. Don Astronaut had a special space suit that kept him alive without food or water or oxygen. One day there was an accident. And Don Astronaut was cast out into space. Don Astronaut orbited the earth and was very scared. Until he remembered his special suit that kept him alive. But nobody's government came to rescue Don Astronaut because it would cost too much money. (There was a con-

> spiracy, and they said he had died, but he hadn't.) So Don Astronaut orbited the earth again and again, fourteen times each day. And Don Astronaut orbited the earth for months. And Don Astronaut orbited the earth for decades. And Don Astronaut orbited the earth for fifty-three years before he died a very lonely and crazy man – just a shell of a thing with hardly a spark for a soul.

When we are separated from God, there is no joy, peace or love. There is only torment.

When we are separated from God, there is no hope. There is only hopelessness.

That is why Jesus' statement on the cross, "My God, my God, why have you forsaken me," is so crucial. The one and only sinless being to walk on earth suffered eternal punishment. He was separated from God for us. No matter what we go through here on earth, no matter what levels of pain, sorrow, or suffering we experience, nothing can compare with being separated from God. Jesus suffered. Not just the betrayals of His best friends, not just the beatings and the torture, not just the humiliation of carrying His cross in front of hundreds of mocking people, and not just the excruciating physical pain of being crucified. Jesus suffered the ultimate: He suffered hell.

In Mel Gibson's movie, The Passion of the Christ, there is a very telling scene at the end of the film. As Jesus is crucified, the sky darkens and the temple splits in half. Just then, the scene shows Satan standing alone, and he is screaming.

What a paradox! The darkest day in history, both here on earth and in heaven provided us with incredible joy, peace, and love.

The darkest day in history also gave us incredible hope. In the end, that is the one and only conclusion.

Before You Go ...

Those of us who suffer through situations like the death of loved ones, terminal illnesses, divorces, or the loss of jobs know how it affects us. However, it is important to remember that we don't live in a vacuum. We are not on our journey alone. Our situation affects so many other people, especially our families.

Because of all the drugs, and the effects of the anesthesia after my surgery, I was in and out of consciousness. My memory of that time is dim, but I was told that my son Alex had asked to see me, alone. He had just turned four-years old. Three years later, I asked my sister if she remembered what happened. I wanted to know and didn't want any more time to go by before she forgot. I was worried the moment could be lost. She e-mailed me this:

> You were in your room in the hospital, after the surgery. I think it was a day or two before you were coming home.
>
> You had asked to see the kids. I think you wanted them to see you before you came home so they kind of knew what was going on. You had the shunt in your head where they had performed surgery. We all kind of explained to the kids that

the shunt was kind of like a band-aid for a cut. It was helping a bad sore heal.

I remember JJ (my best friend from college), Heather (his wife), Dan (my brother), myself, Emily, Alex all being here at this time. JJ and Heather had really been watching and taking care of the kids a lot. Mom, Dee and Christian were there and had left the room. JJ, Heather and Dan left the room and were standing out in the hallway. (Dan might have stayed in the room with me a little longer). Emily was sitting on the bed with you for a little while and Alex was sitting in my lap in the chair next to your bed. He was being very quiet and hardly looking at you. You were sitting up in bed and alert. You were pretty out of it, but able to talk to the kids and ask them questions and tell them that you loved them. Dan left the room with Emily and I think it was just Alex and I left in the room. Alex was still sitting in my lap and he looked at me and said "Aunt Megan can you please leave me alone with my dad?" I said yes, took him down off my lap and got up to give you a kiss and tell you I loved you. When I turned around to leave, Alex was sitting against the wall, on a chair, at the foot of your bed, facing you. While I was in the room, he didn't sit in bed with you. He was sitting with his legs crossed like a pretzel and his hands in his lap. I told him I would wait for him in the hall. He was just looking at you and waiting for me to leave. I think you just said something like "hey buddy" to him as I was leaving the room.

When I went out in the hall, JJ, Heather, Dan and Emily were out there waiting. I told them that Alex had asked me to leave. We were out there for probably about 5 minutes or so. Then the big heavy hospital door to your room slowly opened and Alex walked out. He was kind of looking down at the ground, stone faced. He walked towards all of us, no one really said anything, and without looking up, and without saying a word, he walked to the center of where we were all standing and started to cry. It was a good cry. Heather picked him up and held him. At that point we were all pretty teary eyed.

I remember thinking that from when I left Alex in the room with you, to when he walked out of there by himself, he had just grown up years. He all of a sudden was a little man.

I don't really remember what happened after all that. You had people in and out of your room. No one asked why Alex

> wanted to be alone. I never brought it up, I'm not sure why, I didn't know if it would be hard to talk about or if you would remember. I'm sure Dan and Heather and JJ still remember and have their own version of it.
>
> Anyway, that's what I remember. Sorry if it is hard. It still makes me sad, but it is also such a cool thing. Alex was only 4. That's when he grew up. I love you Mikey and I think of you and pray for you every day. You are an amazing person and I wish I could just take this all away from you. It is not fair that you have to live like this. You just happened to be one of the chosen few that have to live with this craziness. Your strength and faith is a true testament and inspiration.
>
> Love you and miss you.

Alex, being like his father, is a man of few words. A number of years later, he gave us a clue to the fact that he understood. I received confirmation from a project he did in his church class. It said:

> Who is the one person you would like to pray for? My Dad.
>
> God, today, I want to pray for dad. Help him with staying healthy.

More recently, our youngest son Christian surprised us with an interaction he had with a fellow student. His friend's father had been stricken with Multiple Sclerosis, and was confined to a wheelchair. His health was failing quickly. This girl would come to school upset about her father's condition, crying at times. Christian would say to her "Don't worry, my dad has brain cancer and he is still alive. Your dad will be fine." We heard this story from a friend of ours. She said this little girl goes home and tells her parents that our son is one of her best friends. My wife and I were so proud of our son. He was using our situation to help his friend.

In the beginning of my journey, after my radiation treatments, I would get regular MRI's every two months. Over time, they have spaced out to every six months. I was told if everything goes well, they would be conducted once a year. It's great having a goal to shoot for.

Every time I go in for my MRI's, we have the kids pray with us. Even though our kids are at different levels of understanding, they would all be upset if the tumor came back. Everyone would be upset.

I think about this a lot. I am more concerned for my family if God does decide to take me home than for my being taken. This has always been my biggest concern. I want to walk my daughter down the aisle. I want to see my boys venture out into the world. I want to grow old with my wife, travel the country in an RV with our two dogs, and volunteer for the Red Cross. Yet if I am not here to realize those hopes, I want to make sure my family's spiritual life is as strong as it can be.

My mistake is I am not concerned about how they are doing with my situation now. I forget my wife gets more upset after my MRI's are done and come back stable than before. I forget my daughter is trying to lead as normal a life as a teenage girl can. I forget my boys look at me as their father and need me to participate in their lives as much possible. I recognize that I focus too much on the future and not enough on what is going on in my life now.

If you are going through a similar journey, and you know others going through it with you, communication is important. As I write this, I have resolved to talk to all of my kids about my situation and all of the possibilities, and keep talking to them as time goes on.

I have resolved to make sure I understand where my wife is with all of this. Even though I am the one stricken with this disease, I know she has it much more difficult. I appreciate her support, but as her husband, I need to provide support for her, acknowledge her fears and sorrows, and pray to God to help me comfort her.

There are others on this journey with us. They are there for one reason: they love us. We can't forget them. We can't forget how they are feeling. They need our love and support as much as we need theirs.

That is what Christ did. He showed compassion, love and peace to others, even though He knew He was going to suffer.

We can't follow a more perfect example.

So when we wake up in the morning and wonder how in the world we are going to make it, we need to remember one thing: the God of this universe has suffered and that gives us all hope.

I am still navigating this journey that a seven centimeter, malignant, stage four brain tumor has put in my path. Countless MRI's and doctor visits later; I am still living my life.

It is not easy. It is Saturday, after all. To get through this Saturday, one thing is required.

Hope.

A Century of Hope

The feeling is almost surreal. My team has finally arrived, after more than a century of futility, disappointment, heartache and pain.

It is the seventh game of the World Series. My team is ahead by a score of six to three in the top of the ninth inning with three outs to go.

I have dreamt about this day since I was seven years old. It is so incredible; I don't know how to react.

I look to my left, and see my family standing on their feet, yelling and screaming with the rest of the crowd. I turn to the field and realize I have missed the first out of the inning. A pop fly to the right fielder.

One out.

The noise from the crowd is deafening. The next batter up can't concentrate. He is so distracted; he calls time-out twice during his at-bat.

I look down towards Stanley's section in an attempt to seek him out. I can't find him. Odd. He was always there. Why isn't he there now? Why isn't he there on this night?

The crowd roars again. I look back toward the field and realize the distracted batter grounded out four-three.

Two outs.

The crowd at this point has never been louder. I have gone to many games through my lifetime, but I have never heard noise like this. The rafters in the stadium are shaking. Some people have looks of bliss, some joy, and some have tears in their eyes.

One strike.

I look to my left. Stanley is standing next to me.

"Hey kid. Bet you never thought you'd see this day."

"No, I didn't."

Two strikes

"Well here it is. Enjoy it. It's yours."

I turn to Stanley. He is gone.

Strike three. Three outs. It is finally over. Let the celebration begin

Works Cited

Yancey: Philip Yancey, *The Jesus I Never Knew,* Grand Rapids, Zondervan Publishing House, 1995, p. 275.

"The next day": Matthew 27:62-66, The New Jerusalem Bible.

Bell: Rob Bell, *Drops Like Stars,* Grand Rapids, Zondervan, 2009, pp 16-18.

Nouwen: Henri J.M. Nouwen, *The Return Of The Prodigal Son: A Story of Homecoming,* New York, Double day, 1992, p. 13.

Darabont, Frank. <u>The Shawshank Redemption</u>. Warner Brothers, 1994.

Zemeckis, Robert. <u>Contact</u>. Warner Brothers, 1997.

"He went on a little farther": Mark 14: 35-36, New Living Translation.

Shadyac, Tom. <u>Bruce Almighty</u>. Universal Pictures, 2003

Capra, Frank. <u>It's A Wonderful Life</u>. Paramount Pictures, 1946.

Vischer: Phil Vischer, *Me, Myself, & Bob,* Nashville, Thomas Nelson, 2006, pp. 245-246.

Eldredge: John Eldredge, *Walking with God*, Nashville, Thomas Nelson, 2008, pp. 87.

"Therefore do not worry": Matthew 6:34, New International Version.

Stanley: Andy Stanley, *How Good is Good Enough?*, Sisters, Multnoma, 2003, P. 82.

"For I am convinced": Romans 8: 38-39, New International Version.

"When Moses came down": Exodus 34: 29-30, New International Version.

"Soon Levi held a banquet": Luke 5: 29-32, New Living Translation.

"I know I am rotten": Romans 7:18-25, New Living Translation.

Endo: Shusaku Endo, *Silence,* Taplinger, 1969, pp. 171.

"Then Jesus said to them": Matthew 26:31-35, New Jerusalem Bible.

"Meanwhile Peter": Matthew 26: 69-75, New Jerusalem Bible.

Peart: Neil Peart, *Ghost Rider,* Toronto, ECW Press, 2002, p. 62.

"After Job had prayed": Job 42:10, New International Version.

Miller: Donald Miller, *Blue Like Jazz,* Nashville, Thomas Nelson, 2003, pp. 159 – 170.

Gibson, Mel. The Passion of The Christ. Warner Brothers Entertainment, 2004.